OPTIMAL BRAND PERFORMANCE

Leveraging knowledge of why some brands fail and others succeed for building your brand

Published for Emmanuel Obeta

Copyright © 2022 Emmanuel Obeta

For more information on this book or the author:

+234-8139322773
+234-8034007393
Email: eobeta@gmail.com

Printed and Published in the Federal Republic of Nigeria

CONTENTS

ACKNOWLEDGMENTS

Having been exposed to the Coca-Cola and Pepsi Cola brands very early in my career, my interest in Brand Management got a bigger boost on joining the services of Guinness—Diageo, where I was introduced to the concept and process of deliberate and intentional brand building.

My continued pursuit of knowledge in brand management assumed a larger dimension when Mr. Godwin Eze introduced me to Professor Ndolo, who offered me an opportunity to teach brand management to the MBA students of the ESUT Businesses School.

In the course of that lecturing opportunity, I met wonderful people like Mr. Ayo Arowolo, then managing editor of Nigeria's first Financial Newspaper—Financial Standards, who threw open the pages of his newspaper for me to write weekly columns on marketing and brand management.

From there, my curiosity and quest for additional knowledge in brand management became unstoppable. Years later, like a pleasant *de ja vu,* my friend Mr. Steve Omanufeme again offered me another opportunity to maintain a column in the Independent Newspaper on brands and marketing. The result of all that forage into the practice and profession of brand management is the birth of this book, *Optimal Brand Performance.*

Life with its many turns and bumps is a pleasant and intriguing journey where one situation leads to another with circumstances that cannot be said to be remotely connected or profitable, turning out to be the most significant turns and points in the life of a man.

To all who have propelled me on this journey of life, I say a very big thank you. To the numerous adversities I may have faced, I dare say that the unseen hand of God used them all to forge a piece of steel from the raw dust and crucibles of the earth.

To friends and colleagues who have stood by, spicing the journey with fun and heartaches, I remain grateful. To my family, which has been like a Rock of Gibraltar through thick and thin, I cannot say thank you enough. To God most high, who has hidden us in the palms of his hands daily fashioning out the path of our lives and turning the tides in our favor, we daily owe our lives to and cannot thank him enough.

FOREWORD

Marketing is the living discipline that every human being, especially in the evolving economies of the world, is both a participant and benefactor simultaneously. The chief culprit of this phenomenon in marketing is the area of product and branding management. No wonder this new volume on branding—*Optimal Brand Performance*—by an inspired, vastly exposed practitioner and an erudite scholar in the person of Emmanuel Obeta is greatly captivating and promises to exactly optimize your brand, whatever your line of business.

From chapter one, where the author makes you comfortable with the word "brand," he quickly links it up with product and how both relate. He clearly stated the fact that a brand is not a product but is a person's gut feeling about a product, service, or organization. Herein lies wisdom for marketing practitioners and captains of industry at large. Coming to terms with where the product or service starts, the point where the brand becomes imminent, to the point of determining the success or otherwise of the product or service or even the organization as a whole is a critical factor for a competitive edge and survival for the firm.

The book clearly outlines the various features of products and brands. It resonates with the idea that a brand is not just an ordinary attribute of the product or service like all other product attributes but is the very heart or nucleus of any product or service in marketing. This important distinction now portends brand as what drives a product and its market, as well as the organization that owns the brand. Any organization that has not realized this important fact will continue to undervalue and pay lip service to effective branding, whereas an intuitive and insightful business unit will follow through on whatever it takes to optimize its brands in the marketplace.

The rest of the chapters lay out the bedrocks on which successful branding rest. A clear example of what and how branding can be applied to build or re-invigorate ailing brands in an organization is showcased in the concluding "Case Study on Re-branding the Nigerian Police Force."

This book is well written in a language and format anyone can relate with. The lecturers, students, customers, and practitioners will all find it extremely useful. Every serious business faculty, department, and unit needs to have this book in its library in both hard and soft copies.

You are invited to partake of this very practical and inspiring approach to the branding debate. Thank you.

Professor Justie Ody Nnabuko
Professor of Marketing and Director,
Institute of Maritime Studies, UNEC

INTRODUCTION

Every company, organization, or group of people across the world are both enthused and confused by the word "brands" and how to manage them. Several companies have spent millions of dollars to develop unique approaches to creating, building, and managing their brands. The word also has developed an elixir status where every success and failure of the organization and its products or services is attributed to the brand.

Several organizations, as well as industry practitioners, have spent several hours as well as huge amounts of money to find the answer to the critical factors responsible for the successes as well as the failures of brands. This book is merely an attempt to approach the complex field of brand management in a manner that seeks to demystify and clarify the concept of brands and what any brand practitioner should know about the key indices responsible for the success and failures of their brands.

Watching through the years the huge successes made by brands like Coca-Cola, Pepsi Cola, Mercedes Benz, Apple, Microsoft, Harley Davidson Motorcycles, and several others too numerous to mention, one cannot but wonder what the basic ingredients of their successes are; how they have been able to consistently over the years and across several continents and countries build such a long-lasting legacy of brands laced with a litany of remarkable moments and huge connect with their customers. These are the major thoughts at the heart of this book; an expedition through the successes and failures of several brands as well as the causative factors for such successes and failures.

Reference is made all across the book to the major insights and thoughts of prominent authors and trailblazers in the field of brand management, just like the famous saying, "If I am standing tall today, it is merely because I stood on the shoulders of several others who had gone before us."

The book, in its journey, started with an attempt to understand and clarify the meaning and origin of the word "brands," the basic differences between a brand and a product or service. From there, it looked at the different types of brands as well as the architecture of these brands or how they have been organized over the years. From there, the book then took a leap into an exploratory study of several brands and the various factors responsible for their successes and failures.

Brand management, like every other field of human endeavor or field of study, is made up of several building blocks that, if assembled in the right order and proportion, will result in the building of a strong edifice or field of study. The book looked at some of these building blocks like differentiation, distinctiveness, salience as well as brand positioning, brand identity, etc. Without a good measurement parameter, it will definitely be impossible to assess the level of progress made in any field of life. In the same way, all the efforts expended in building a brand cannot be said to have succeeded if there are no parameters, standards, or benchmarks that these efforts can be measured against, so the book dwelt a bit on the various types of measurement parameters for the brand; brand equity and all that.

Finally, we tried to juxtapose all these concepts and principles to a real-life case study of an organization—the police force, which all across the world not only in Nigeria can benefit hugely from the principles enunciated by brand management in refocusing, repackaging, and re-presenting itself to the populates that they seek to protect so as to enjoy their confidence and goodwill. It is our hope that the book would have at least answered some of the basic questions agitating the minds of several brand practitioners and also contributed in any small way to the existing body of knowledge in brand management.

CHAPTER ONE

What Is a Brand?

According to Roland Barthes, meaning can be elusive; it flows and drifts and is often hard to pin down. Regardless of that, it still remains an endless search engraved in the heart of man. Meaning is also not manufactured or cast in concrete, nor is it a given; it is up for negotiation and interpretation, and the individual plays an active role in the very creation of this meaning.

In trying to define or arrive at the meaning of brands, the best place to start will be the history and origin of brands. Branding arguably commenced in ancient Egypt, where brick makers were said to have put symbols on their bricks to identify them. In Europe, the earliest signs of branding were the medieval guilds' efforts to require craftsmen and craftswomen to put trademarks on their products to protect themselves and consumers against imitation and inferior quality. In the United States, cattle ranchers would brand their livestock to more easily identify them. Manufacturers began to burn their identities onto the barrels that carried their products using a branding iron. The Guinness harp and the Bass red triangle are among the world's oldest registered trademarks, being first registered in 1876.

In defining the term brands, so many people have come up with different definitions or explanations as to what their own understanding of the term means.

The Economist defined a brand as a name given to a product and/or service such that it takes on an identity by itself. This forces us to ask a series of questions. For example, what is in a name? Does a name have any intrinsic meaning or significance? Can a name standing alone make any meaning, or are there things one has to imbue or embed in a name to make it attain or acquire significance? What is the concept of meaning, and how do you arrive at meaning? In today's marketplace teeming with thousands of products and services, all of which are being rapidly commoditized, how can a name as a brand make it stand out from the clutter and attract attention or gain the required identity?

The American Marketing Association went further in its definition of a brand in 1960 to introduce some other elements into the concept of a brand. It defined a brand as "A name, term, sign, symbol, or design, or a combination of them, intended to identify the goods or services of one seller or group of sellers and to differentiate them from those of competitors." By this definition, they emphasized visual features as a means of identification and brand differentiation.

John Sherry went further to expatiate on this definition. According to him, three basic clusters of meaning have emerged based on the chronological account of the birth and development as well as the evolving changes in form and meaning (etymology) of the word brand. The first one clusters around the concept of 'burning' with connotations of guardianship, custodianship, family origin, or roots. The second one relates to 'marking' which has connotations of ownership, indelibility, and an allusion to an intrinsic essence (something it has and unique to it which no other brand has or can have), and the third cluster centers around the "delivery or deliverance from danger, imitation or faking"). Other definitions of the brand also followed in very quick successions and from diverse sources as follows.

A brand is akin to a living being: it has an identity and personality, name, culture, vision, emotion, and intelligence. All these are conferred by the owner of the brand and need to be continuously looked at to keep the brand relevant to the target it intends to sell to.

A brand is a product, service, person, company, or a concept that has characteristics like a name, symbol, etc., which can be differentiated from others in the market. It is what makes the product identifiable and differentiable.
A brand is the combination of properties within and outside a product, which gives an identity to the generic product. It cannot be separated from the product.

Central to all these definitions is the purpose intended to be achieved by the branding effort like differentiation, identity, relevance, etc. The definitions also expressly imply an active process of building these characteristics into the product by the brand owner, which then becomes the vehicular mode of expressing these inbuilt characteristics.

> *"...a brand encapsulates in its name and its visual symbol all the goodwill created by the positive experiences of clients or prospects with the organization, its products, its channels, its stores, its communication and its people."*

David Aaker, however, pointed out one huge anomaly in some of these definitions of the brand, which is that it has been framed as a cognitive and structural enterprise by strategic marketing, thereby overlooking the lived experience that consumers have of brands. Marketers, according to John Sherry, are behavioral architects or social engineers who, in conjunction with consumers, public policymakers, and consumerists, are involved in the never-ending game of discovering, creating, translating, transforming, and reconfiguring meaning which is the primary quest that drives the marketplace behavior.

Brands, according to him, are therefore essential ingredients in this equation because they are the principal repositories of meaning in the consumer culture both as a storehouse and as a powerhouse. A brand, according to John Sherry, is therefore not a differentiator alone but also a promise, a license to charge a premium, a mental shortcut that discourages rational thought, an infusing with the spirit of the maker, a performance, a gathering, an inspiration, a contract, a relationship, a guarantee, an elastic covenant with loose rules of engagement, a hologram of the firm, etc.
Brand, according to him, can also be looked at as a habitat that consumers can be induced to dwell in, domesticate the space, transforming it and themselves, to the extent that the resultant glows emanating from the dwelling place is the brand's aura. It is also a physical and metaphysical presence, an economic and festive fixture that binds stakeholders in a multifaceted relationship.

The definition of what a brand is eventually moved from the tangible toward the intangible for instance David Ogilvy, the "Father of Advertising," defined a brand as the intangible sum of a product's attributes. Marty Neumeier, on the other hand, defined brand by first laying out what a brand is not: "A brand is not a logo. A brand is not an identity. A brand is not a product. "a brand, according to him, is a person's gut feeling about a product, service, or organization." This feeling or gut feeling is resident within the enclaves of the individual's mind and is owned by the individual and personal to him or her.

"Ignyte" defined a brand as the way a company, organization, or individual is perceived by those who experience it. More than simply a name, term, design, or symbol, a brand is the recognizable feeling a product or business evokes.
Brands, then, live in the mind. They live in the minds of everyone who experiences them: employees, investors, the media, and, perhaps most importantly, customers.

Jerry McLaughlin defined a brand as what your prospect thinks of when he or she hears your brand name. It's everything the public thinks it knows about your name brand offering—both factual and emotional. He went further to point out that your brand name exists objectively; people can see it. It's fixed. But your brand exists only in someone's mind.

These definitions throw up the issue of perception, feelings, emotions, memory, associations, the consumer's minds—what they think about you, your product, organization, etc. How then does a brand move from being a name, logo, etc., and transmogrify into something that resides in the mind?

Just as it is prevalent in every communication activity, the famous SMCR model of communication and the Intervening variables school comes into effect. Some are of the opinion that the process of the brand creation is entirely the resultant effect of the various marketing activities initiated by the marketer or owner of the brand (the SMCR approach), whereas others are of the opinion that certain intervening variables domiciled within the ambit of the consumer and his environment play a vital role in the formation process for the brand.

According to Kapferer, although communication is necessary to create a brand, it is far from being sufficient. Certainly, a brand encapsulates in its name and its visual symbol all the goodwill created by the positive experiences of clients or prospects with the organization, its products, its channels, its stores, its communication, and its people.

Mark Batey is also of the same opinion that a brand is created, not only as a result of a marketer's activities (the stimulus or "input") but also, critically, as a result of the consumer's reading of and reaction to those activities (the "take-out"). For instance, from the marketer's perspective, a brand is a promise, a covenant; however, from the consumer's perspective, it is the set of associations, perceptions, and expectations existing in his or her mind.

Brand associations are created, sustained, and enhanced by every experience and encounter a consumer has with the brand. A TV commercial is an encounter with the brand. So is the act of using or physically consuming it. These experiences and encounters with the brand over time build up into collections of associations, influencing brand perceptions and forming a brand associative network or brand engram.

Engrams, according to Daniel Schachter, are "the transient or enduring changes in our brains that result from encoding an experience such that from a neuropsychological perspective, a brand is "the totality of stored synaptic connections. These connections between brand associations are reinforced over time, and they effectively come to define the brand in the consumers' minds.

Following from all these, Mark Batey arrived at a definition of brand as a cluster of meanings. These meanings and their nature evolve over time such that without brand meanings, there is no brand. McCracken also agrees with this position, such that, according to him, "Brands are first and foremost a bundle of meanings without which it will not be possible to talk about brand images, brand personalities, or brand positions. Crafting brand experiences are just a means of communicating brand meanings.

Mark Batey went further to point out that brands are about relationships also. It, therefore, follows that since people's mental associations are the basic foundations of brands, the stronger the consumer's mental associations with the brands are, the stronger the intricate relationship with the brand will be. Brands therefore flourish or die based on the strength of these relationships. This bond of relationship with particular brands is also what leads to consumer loyalty. Relationships are also in themselves about trust.

Despite all the above definitions of the brand, Kapferer introduced a new element into the definition of the brand. According to him, Brands are intangible assets, assets that produce added benefits for the business. He pointed out two major paradigms in the various definitions of the brand. The first one is customer-based, which focuses exclusively on the customer's relationship with the brand, which ranges from the point of total indifference to attachment, loyalty, and willingness to buy and rebuy based on beliefs of superiority and evoked emotions. The other paradigm is the one that aims at producing financial measures in dollars, euros, or yen.

The financial approach measures the value of the brand by isolating the net additional cash flows created by the brand. These additional cash flows are the result of customers' willingness to buy one brand more than its competitors, even when another brand is cheaper. The customers' rationale for wanting to pay more for these particular brands is based on the beliefs and bonds that have been created over time in their minds through the marketing of the brand. In other words, customer equity is the preamble of financial equity. Brands have financial value because they have created assets in the minds and hearts of customers, distributors, prescribers, and opinion leaders.

These assets, according to him, are brand awareness, beliefs of exclusivity and superiority of some valued benefits, emotional bonding, etc. which are what Keller alluded to in his definition of a brand; that "a brand is a set of mental associations, held by the consumer, which add to the perceived value of a product or service." His only problem with the definition is that the product or service, the prime vector of the perceived value, is left out of the scope of the brand definition, thereby rendering the function of managing the brand as only a communication task.

According to him, the financial perspective helps us adequately define brands and brand equity, especially as brands are both intangible and conditioned assets that deliver benefits over a long period of time working in consonance with other material assets like production facilities. The product for him is, therefore, an embodiment of the brand by which the brand becomes real. The product also is the main source of the brand's valuation—whether it produces high or low satisfaction. Brand management, therefore, commences with the creation of products, services, and/or places that embody the brand.

Following from all the above definitions of the brand, certain facts become very clear. One is that Brand is a very complex phenomenon with each expert coming up with his or her own definition, understanding, or perspective of the concept such that there has not been a commonality or agreement of what the definition of the concept is or should be.

Secondly is that brands are both ubiquitous and omnipresent, cutting across every facet of life: economic, social, cultural, religious, sporting, etc. such that according to Kapferer, a good definition or understanding of the concept must come from a multifaceted or multi-disciplinary analysis covering both macroeconomics; microeconomics, sociology, anthropology, history, semiotics, philosophy, etc.

Chernatony and Riley, in their seminal work, classified the definitions of a brand into twelve themes, namely; brand as a logo, brand as a legal instrument, brand as a company, brand as a shorthand, brand as a risk reducer, brand as an Identity system, brand as an image in consumer's mind, brand as a value system, brand as a personality, brand as relationship, brand as adding value and brand as an evolving entity which in effect represents the entirety of the various definitions of the concept.

In summary, after browsing through all the various definitions of brand, five key elements that represent or must be present so as to have a composite definition of the concept are as follows.

Brands encompass some physical or visual elements such as a name, logo, product, service, company, or an individual. There is also the mental, cognitive and emotional dimension of the brand that resides in the heart and mind of the consumers (the feelings, perceptions, emotions, attitudes, associations, etc.). The third dimension is the purpose or objective in seeking to create or give birth to such a brand—the economic and other rationales. The creation process of the brand as initiated by the marketers and the brand owners is the fourth dimension and, finally, the modification process that is responsible for the final nature of the brand, either intended, deliberate, or unintended. This modification process comes as a result of the interaction between the brand and the consumers and the resultant experience.

A composite definition of the brand that is representative of all the essential dimensions of the brand must incorporate all these key elements and not any of these single processes standing alone on its own.

CHAPTER TWO

What Is a Product and Its Relationship with the Brand?

Marty Neumeier, in defining a brand, first laid out what a brand is not. According to him,

"A brand is not a logo. A brand is not an identity. A brand is not a product; rather a brand is a person's gut feeling about a product, service, or organization."

Kapferer, in his definition of a brand, pointed out the illuminating differences between a product and a brand. According to him, you buy a product for what it does while you choose a brand for what it means. A product sits on the retailers' shelves, whereas a brand exists in the consumers' minds. A product can be quickly outdated, whereas a brand is timeless. A product can be copied by a competitor, whereas a brand is unique and defies copying.

A product, therefore, becomes or attains the status of a brand when the physical product is augmented by something else—images, symbols, perceptions, feelings, etc.—to produce an integral idea greater than the sum of its parts. This, for example, is the reason why Pepsi in a blind test can be preferred over Coca-Cola several times over, but the trend changes once the actual brand names of the product and their packaging are introduced.

A brand might be composed of a single product, or it might be made up of multiple products that span many categories. But at its core, there remains a soul, distinctive identity and image that resonates with its consumers and transcends its physical representation in terms of product format like Mercedes Benz, Jaguar, etc.

It will also be pertinent to ask or try to find out in the sequence of things which one comes first, a product or a brand? In trying to answer that question, let's find out more about what a product really is. The Oxford Dictionary defined a product as an article or substance that is manufactured or refined for sale or a thing or person that is the result of an action or process.

According to the Economic Times of India, a product is what is offered for sale. It can be a service or an item. It can be physical or in a virtual or cyber form. Whatever its form, a product is made at a cost, and each is sold at a price. The price that can be charged depends on the market, the quality, the marketing, and the segment that is targeted.

Wikipedia defined a product as an object or system made available for consumer use; it is anything that can be offered to a market to satisfy the desire or need of a customer. In retailing, products are often referred to as merchandise, while in manufacturing, products are bought as raw materials and then sold as finished goods.

A product becomes or attains the status of a brand when the physical product is augmented by something else—images, symbols, percep-

A product can therefore be classified as tangible or intangible. A tangible product is a physical object that can be perceived by touch, such as a building, vehicle, or gadget. Most goods are tangible products. For example, a soccer ball is a tangible product.

An intangible product, on the other hand, is a product that can only be perceived indirectly, such as an insurance policy. Intangible data products can further be classified into virtual digital goods ("VDG"), which are virtually located on a computer OS and accessible to users as conventional file types, such as JPG and MP3 files. Virtual digital goods require further application processing or transformational work by programmers, so their use may be subject to license and or rights of digital transfer. On the other hand, real digital goods ("RDG") may exist within the presentational elements of a data program independent of a conventional file type.

Products in whatever their different states exist basically to meet the needs of the customers. Customers on their own have three different ways or drivers, which enable them to attach value to a product; their need (the lack of a basic requirement), their want (a specific requirement for a product or service to meet a need), and their demand (a set of wants plus the desire and ability to pay for the product which will, in turn, meet the need that they have).

The choice of a particular product is therefore based on a nexus of these values and the perceived value of the product to live up to their expectations. Satisfaction or dissatisfaction is therefore based on the ability of the product to meet up or live up to these expectations at the point of usage.

Five Different Levels of Products Existence

Products, according to Kotler, exist at five different levels and can best be understood at these five different levels of what should make up a product offering. The core benefit represents the fundamental need or want that consumers satisfy by consuming the product or service. For example, the core benefit of Coca-Cola and most other drinks is to quench a thirst or mobility for automobiles.

The second level is the generic product devoid of any embellishments or upgrades; the basic level or version of the product containing only those attributes or characteristics absolutely necessary for it to function; the knocked down version of the product. For a car, this will be the basic functionality required for the car to move from one point to another.

The expected product is the third level and represents the set of attributes or characteristics that buyers normally expect and agree to when they purchase a product. For instance, a drink is expected to be served cold so as to effectively quench thirst, whereas a sports car is expected to have a certain level of inbuilt speed, performance, and maneuverability to function as a sports car.

The augmented product involves the inclusion of additional features, benefits, attributes, or related services that serve to differentiate the product from its competitors and position it in a class of its own. This will refer to all the available options that can be included in a Mercedes 500 to customize it and differentiate it from Mercedes 350 etc.

The potential product is the fifth level and represents all the augmentations and transformations a product might undergo in the future. This is important because not only do customers' expectations and values change with time, but businesses must aim to surprise and delight customers in the future by continuing to augment products so as to be able to retain their loyalty. A lot of scenario buildings and forecasting will be required to arrive at the possible future state of the product that will be desirable to the customers.

The five levels of the product, therefore, provide veritable tools or platforms that can be manipulated to be able to build a strong brand. The brand triangle concept can be used in trying to build a product brand as follows;

What concept should one choose, and with what balance of tangible and intangible benefits, as well as the particular level of product, should one settle for in designing the identity and positioning of the brand?

How should the brand concept be embodied in its products or services? How should a product or service of the brand be different, look different? What products can this brand concept encompass, or what will be the boundary beyond which a particular product cannot extend or be stretched so as not to lose its distinctiveness? For example, what will be the limit of Mercedes 350 in its brand evolution so as to still remain distinct and different from all other Mercedes products while still being focused or positioned for the particular segment for which it is being targeted?

The Brand Triangle

The Brand Triangle is one approach you can use to distinctly identify and position products or services. In seeking to build a lasting product or service brand, three key components must be taken into consideration; the brand platform to be created, customer experience or emotions, and the product strategy.

When all these are put together, according to Dessinger and Thelen, your brand will be strong and possess an all-rounded appeal for your target customers. The role of your brand platform is to articulate your persona, how you are meaningfully different in the marketplace (your differentiation)—what you do differently from anyone else in your industry, and why it's better. Your customer experience, on the other hand, needs to establish an emotional connection—how you want your customers to feel whenever and wherever they interact with you.

Your product strategy, on the other hand, needs to deliver utility and value—what are they actually spending money on? What needs it meets. Where your product fits on the quality and price dimensions vs. their alternatives, and how does it create superior value in the marketplace?

At the center of the triangle is the customer, mainly because whatever you do or think, it is the customer's perspective of those things you have done, not what you think about them, that matters. You may have thought that you have arrived at a eureka moment, whereas the customer may not think too highly about that. An example could be a particular augmentation to the product, which, based on your perspective, will be a deal clincher; meanwhile, the customer may not think too highly or be particularly enthused by them.

Targeting, therefore, is a key element of this customer experience design because what certain segments of the market might be enthused about might be a put-off for the other segment. A very good understanding of the target segment is therefore paramount so as to discover what appeals and what does not appeal to them.

The three elements of the triangle are mutually reinforcing to each other. The product strategy, for instance, is tightly connected to the desired customer service experience. The customer experience, in turn, rides on the back of the product strategy; what you want the product to accomplish or your vision about what you want the product to be, achieve or represent for the customer as well as within its product category is what at the end of the day will determine the possible range of experiences and outcomes that the customers can have with your product.

The platform is, therefore, the glue that holds the entire triangle together as well as provides a point of view, opinion, or perspective for the product or brand. The platform is also the creative process that neatly designs and ties all these points (the customer experience and the product strategy) together so as to present to the customers a meaningfully impactful brand that can resonate with their psyche; something that they will want to own and to hold or be identified with as a means of fulfilling their innate desires as well as expressing it.

One can also safely say that the product strategy encompasses the popular 4Ps of marketing. The product offering, the price position or point that you want the product to hold in the market; the promotional strategy for the product as well as the distribution strategy for the product—what kinds of outlets you will want the product distributed through as well as the kinds of people—distributors that you will want involved in the distribution of the products.

The customer experience, among other things, will incorporate the people that the product is targeted at, the promise the product/brand is making to them, as well as the personality, trait, or perspective being propagated by the product/brand. This is critical because not every product is targeted at every customer. Dove, Oil of Olay, etc., are all types of soaps or body lotions targeted at a completely different set of people from Lux soaps or Pears body lotion.

So the actual question becomes, do you first produce a product and then seek to brand it, or do you first design a brand and then seek to produce products that represent or carry or represent the brand.

Based on our discussion so far, a product will take some time and pass through some processes before it becomes identified with some cherished images, symbols, perceptions, feelings by the consumers or before it connotes an idea or ideal that is cherished or held dear by the consumers. Consequently, a product will naturally exist first in terms of its offering before it grows to represent some other intangible ideals that resonate with the consumer.

However, a lot of strategic marketing and brand management techniques have been deployed to ensure that from concept design, production, and packaging, the product is positioned to occupy a place in the minds of the consumers or to represent some ideals from day one. This short-circuits the process or the time required for the product to assume the status of a brand. A clear path is designed for the product in its journey or evolution so as to save it from happenstance or the vagaries of uncertainties or chance that may befall it. With careful management of the various indices, the product achieves the desired status faster in a determined manner rather than through a process of luck or chance.
In conclusion, a product is made by a company and can be purchased by a consumer in exchange for money, while brands are built through consumer perceptions, expectations, and experiences with all the products or services under a brand umbrella. For example, Toyota's product is cars. Its umbrella brand is Toyota, and each product has its own more specific brand name to distinguish the various Toyota-manufactured product lines from one another. Without a product, there is no need for a brand.

According to Susan Gunelius, there are several fundamental differences between a brand and a product (or a service), although popular products can *become* brands unto themselves while brand names can be used to refer to products.

> **At the center of the triangle is the customer mainly because whatever you do or think it is the customer's perspective of those things you have done not what you think about them that matter.**

A product can be copied by competitors at any time. When Amazon launched the Kindle e-reader device, it didn't take long for competitors to come out with their own branded versions of an e-reader product. However, the brand associated with each e-reader device offers unique value based on the perceptions, expectations, and emotions that consumers develop for those brands through previous experiences with them.

Similarly, a product can be replaced with a competitor's product if consumers believe the two products offer the same features and benefits. Products with low emotional involvement are typically easily replaced.

Products can become obsolete, but brands can be timeless such that the memories of such brands still linger in the mind of the consumers long after it has ceased being an economic item. An example is a goody-goody sweet, which was a strong brand years ago. Though it has ceased to exist, most people who liked the sweet as kids still do have fond memories about it, and its brand equity still remains very strong. VHS players are another good example of obsolete brands.

A product will take some time and pass through some processes before it becomes identified with some cherished images symbols, percep- tions, feelings by the consumers or before it connotes an idea or ideal that is cherished or held dear by the consumers.

Products are instantly meaningful, but brands become meaningful over time. When you launch a new product, it's easy to make that product instantly meaningful and useful to consumers because it serves a specific function for them. However, a brand is mean- ingless until consumers have had a chance to experience it, build trust with it, and believe in it. It takes time and effort to convince consumers to believe in your brand.

Consider Google as an example. When Google first hit the internet scene, it offered a simple product—a search engine. That product was instantly meaningful to consumers because it helped them find information online quickly. However, the Google brand didn't become meaningful to consumers until people had a chance to use the Google search engine product and see for themselves that it really was a better search engine. Through those experi- ences, consumers began to trust that the Google brand could deliver faster and better information online. Today, when Google launches a new product (like Google+ recently), people are quick to try those products because they trust the Google brand.

CHAPTER THREE

Brand Architecture and Different Types of Brands

Human beings, in the process of trying to make a meaning about their lives, codify, organize, group, and store their knowledge, experience, perception, feelings, emotions, memory, and associations with different things, objects, places, and events that they come across or interact with. Such that when similar issues or circumstances arise or crop up in the future, they do not go through the entire process of evaluating or analyzing those events afresh before making a decision about them but will rather pull up their stored memory of previous experiences with those objects so as to inform their current decisions and opinions about those events.

These experiences, if consistently reinforced, become a strong enough impetus to guide an individual's actions and impressions about those decision objects, whereas others may not assume any level of significance and, as such, are left simmering in the subconscious.

For those that assume a certain level of significance or that the owners will want to consciously turn a brand into a profitable asset that has the potential of influencing public opinion or perception and even possibly earn some returns, their range is diverse and many. The object of some of these pleasurable encounters has the potentiality of becoming brands.

Organizations, by their nature, may have motley brands or just a single brand. However, in real life, it is difficult to find an organization with just a single brand. Organizations usually try to build brands in the various areas or segments of the market that they wish to serve so as to ensure complete coverage of the selected markets that they seek to serve.

Brands, by their very nature, are very complex and ubiquitous in nature. Brand architecture is, therefore, a means whereby the organization seeks to organize its numerous brands into a system that is coherent, makes sense, and is mutually reinforcing. According to Steve Gilman, brand architecture is a system that organizes brands, products, and services to help an audience access and relate to a brand. It also enables consumers to form opinions and preferences for an entire family of brands by interacting or learning about only one brand in that family.

The brand architecture ensures that each separate brand from the collectivity of brands from the same umbrella carries with it an integral element, DNA, trademark, or pointer that boosts and reinforces the other brands within the family of brands. It is just like a family tree that gives birth to several children who behave like siblings, for instance, cousins or in-laws that all have the same family traits.

It is also an important guide for brand extensions, sub-brands, and the development of new products as it provides a boundary for each set of brands by defining what can be accommodated within the brand concept and what should exist beyond the boundaries of the brand.

New products, innovations, and ideas for new products will always arise, but the key question in trying to make sense out of these new products or brand concepts are what products can be similarly branded as belonging within the same subset of needs and what products will be impossible or difficult to fit into the same needs segment such that any attempt to fit such products or its enhancements into the same needs class will lead to a loss of meaning, synergy, and coherence for such brands as to what they actually represent.

For example, Toyota, in its quest to play and occupy a sizeable chunk of the luxurious car segment, had to come up with a new brand Lexus, as there is a limit to how far the brand name Toyota can be extended within the market without losing its value or sense of identity. Toyota, in its branding, capitalized on the rugged, reliable, resilient, and optimum performance segment of the market for all their brands. As much as all these are useful, luxury does not necessarily derive from these elements and, as such, cannot be credibly extended into the high-end luxury segment of the auto market hence the need for a completely new brand that can benefit from the family or group aura of quality but specifically positioned for the luxury end of the market.

Brand architecture, therefore, provides a road map for brand identity development and design while reminding consumers of the value proposition for the entire brand family, thereby ensuring that the maximum brand value is achieved by fully leveraging both corporate and sub-brands.

Brand architecture, according to Marshall, considers all products and services to be part of a continuum, attracting a community of like-minded audiences, with nuanced differences between them; a big circle that grows as products and services are added to it.

The benefit of this approach is that an audience or customer base may be brought into the community by any one of these brands, and they are subsequently exposed to more and more of the other brands within the family, thereby building the strength and influence of the parent identity.

> *Brands by their very nature are very complex and ubiquitous in nature. Brand architecture is therefore a means whereby the organization seeks to organize their numerous brands into a system that is coherent, makes sense and is mutually reinforcing.*

According to Derek Smith, brand architecture is one veritable way of trying not to confuse the marketplace about what products and services that your company offers. This is especially important for companies that have been in business for a long time and have grown through acquisitions, acquiring both new and legacy brands with their own separate brand identities, thereby turning them into multi-layers of the brand mix.

Brand architecture, therefore, is a way of organizing the different subsections of a larger brand by showing us how they all relate to each other. It is beneficial to the marketer as it can help him see how to keep parts of a brand separate when needed and also how to allow them to work together to boost one another in the marketplace.

For Marshall, brand architecture is basically about the relationships between a parent identity and all of its products, divisions, and services, which help determine the role of the parent and the role of the individual pieces in the overall organizational strategy. If the organization's goal is to be known as one single, powerful entity (Like Google, FedEx, or Virgin), it will create a very tight relationship between it and all its products, services, and divisions, but if its goal is to let its products and services multiply and succeed independently of each other, it might opt for looser relationship.

Types of Brand Architecture

There are three main types of brand architecture, namely, the branded house, the house of brands, and the endorsed brand.

The branded house or the "corporate dominant," according to Marshall, is a situation where the parent identity establishes a very tight relationship between itself and its products and services such that it uses the parent identity to form a strong community of closely related services where the more a user enjoys their experience with one service, the more likely they are to try another thereby leading to increased strength or brand equity of the corporate brand. Google, Virgin, and FedEx are good examples of this approach. This structure, according to Derek Smith, makes for a consistent experience, minimizes confusion, and builds equity for the corporate brand.

The house of brands or the product dominant brand architecture is a situation where the parent identity takes a backseat or even a non-visible presence in favor of its individual product and service brands. Here the parent brand exists, but it's not reflected in the sub-brands in an obvious or blatant way and is often in the background, overshadowed by one or more of its sub-brands. This brand architecture model is more prevalent in situations where a holding company buys up subsidiaries—to most consumers, the parent company is irrelevant compared to the individual products that it distributes.

Procter & Gamble and Microsoft are good examples of this approach. In this approach, each of the product lines is allowed to thrive independently and even compete against each other because they represent distinctly different promises. While this model enables lots of independence, it can also lead to brand proliferation and high marketing costs. Consequently, a house of brands, according to Marshall, is a much more expensive route that favors the independence of its individual products or divisions but diminishes the importance and visibility of the parent identity.

The hybrid or endorsing brand is a more flexible way to package brands under a master brand. Brand extensions are given separate identities and are associated with the master brand, or not, depending on the context. This gives you the freedom to have independent strategies for the brand extensions but also to use the equity of the master brand when it's convenient. A good example is Harp from the Guinness—Diageo group.

At the end of the day, brand architecture is a strategic tool deployed to achieve the organization's goal or objective and not just a fad or fashion adopted to suit the proclivities of certain individuals. Brand architecture, according to Marshall, should therefore be systemic—with a thought about what you are trying to accomplish overall, how many distinct promises you need to make to grow your business, and how many individual brands you can afford to support. Thinking this through at a high level will help you better understand and activate the roles of each brand in your overall strategy.

Types of Brands

Despite the ubiquitous, overarching, and complex nature of brands, there are ways of categorizing them into categories that can be broadly representative of all brands.

Many marketing professionals have adopted different ways of classifying brands, like Mark di Somma who believes that there are twenty-one different categories or classifications of brands based on the role that the brands play and the nature of the brands. Dennise Lee Yohn, on the other hand, believes that there are only nine different kinds of brands based on the different strategies, stances, or approaches that brands take in shaping their identity and positioning. For him, regardless of the nature of the brands, if the modality or mechanics adopted in building the brands are the same, then they all fall into the same category regardless of the nature or the roles that they play.

In adopting Mark Di Somma's perspective, there are twenty-one types of brands, and they are as follows;

Corporate or institutional brands serve to describe an organization as a whole with the intention of creating a consistent corporate image for the organization through the interplay of corporate strategy, business activity, and the entire corporate function materials. The corporate brand embodies a set of values and takes on an orientation that addresses and positions the organization across its major stakeholders, influence, and target groups, inclusive of their employees. These values and corporate culture, vision, and mission provide a unique rallying point and differentiation for the organization that distinguishes it from all organizations. The corporate brand could be a single brand company like Apple or a multi-brand company like Samsung, Unilever, etc.

Corporate brands, according to Greyser and Urde, serves as a beacon whose purpose is to provide direction and purpose while breathing life and license to operate or exist for the individual products within its portfolio. It helps firms recruit and retain employees, enhances the image of the products under its umbrella, and provides protection against reputational damage for both the organization and its products in times of trouble. According to David Aaker, "The corporate brand defines the firm that will deliver and stand behind the offering that the customer will buy and use."

The employer brand, according to William Tincup, is the company's ability to differentiate and promote its unique identity (the feeling, culture, and experience that pervades the organization) to a defined group of candidates that are in the employment market or that are interested in being hired.

Employer branding is basically a subset of the corporate or institutional brand with a specific focus on the employment market geared toward presenting the organization as the employer of choice to the category of employees that the organization needs, wants to attract, recruit and retain. It is also a part of the employee value proposition, the promise you make to employees in exchange for their experience, talents, contacts, and skills.

It is viewed as a second brand that is related to your primary brand and majorly about how you are viewed as an employer, which according to Sarah Lybrand, lives and breathes in the minds and hearts of your former, current, and future employees. The key in employer branding is the ability to create fulfillment, excitement, and a sense of purpose for your employees, coupled with the ability to make such visible to all potential or future employees.

The investor brand, which can safely be said to be an aspect of the corporate or institutional brand, according to Designate, is usually critical for listed companies whose market capitalization in large part are composed of 'intangibles' that are intertwined with the out-workings of 'brand'; and, which are subject to swift and sometimes lasting retribution from consumers, regulators and investors when things go wrong.

For them, investor branding is therefore about structured long-term engagement with the market, which enables the company to define for itself how it is perceived. It paints a picture of the future and how to get there, which makes the investor feel more secure as well as builds trust among them both in the safety of their investments as well as the competence of the people managing them. This builds a buffer around the business and its financial performance while creating and earning the goodwill required for it to operate.

The confidence created by the Investor brand among the investing public is the most valuable asset in times of crisis as the investors will want to be assured of the company's admixture of long term strategy and tactics to maximize profits both in the short term and in the long term.

Non-Governmental Organization (NGO) or non-profit brand: these two are generally classified as the same in most countries, with the only difference being in the scope of work or causes that NGOs adopt, which can be broader and sometimes with international footprints.

Most of these organizations adopt brand management as a tool for raising funds. However, a growing number are broadening the scope of managing their brands to include driving broad, long-term social goals while strengthening internal identity, cohesion, and capacity. Some like Amnesty International, Habitat for Humanity, Red Cross Society, etc., have successfully transitioned into this second phase where social impact and organizational cohesion are the more desirable focus for the organizations.

Activist brand and brand activism: although composed of the same words, the two are worlds apart in meaning and approach. The major difference lies in the major purpose or objective of the brand. Some brands like Black Lives Matter, by their major conception, are activist brands as they are built or formulated with a clear and major objective of fighting for a cause; that is, their life or raison d' etre. Some other brands like Nike can wake up to support a cause like a campaign against child labor or low payment of wages for workers. That approximates to brand activism and does not make Nike an activist brand. This can be likened to the argument between the hen and the pig on the making of an omelet and ham. To make a ham, the pig has to be killed, but for the omelet, all that needs to happen will be for the hen to lay some eggs.

Brand activism, according to activistbrands.com **consists of business efforts that promote, impede, or direct social, political, economic, and/or environmental reform or stasis with the desire to promote or impede improvements in society.**

Brand activism is an evolution beyond the values-driven corporate social responsibility and environmental, social, and governance programs. It is basically an attempt to align the company's values with the values of their customers, their employees, and society at large by adopting an outside-in approach where the organization tries to wear the shoe so as to see where it pinches.

Personal brands, according to personalbrand.com, are a widely recognized and largely uniform perception or impression of an individual based on their experience, expertise, competencies, actions, and/or achievements within a community, industry, or the marketplace at large. Whereas personal branding is the conscious and intentional effort to create and influence public perception of an individual by positioning them as an authority in their industry, elevating their credibility, and differentiating themselves from the competition, to ultimately advance their career, increase their circle of influence, and have a larger impact.

The process of personal branding, therefore, involves identifying your area of uniqueness, building a reputation around it, and getting known for it up to a point where such reputation can be monetized, an admixture of self-improvement and self-packaging.

Personal brands can refer to an individual like Bill Gates or a collectivity of individuals whose identity is as a collectivity and not as individuals. Outside of the group, they do not have an identity or assume a completely different identity other than that of the group. A good example is the Nigerian musical group P-Square, who, as a group of twins, had a personal brand P-Square but, on break up, assumed a completely different identity as neither could assume the P-Square brand anymore.

Celebrity brands: these are basically personal brands that have achieved some high level of fame or popularity either as a result of continuous appearances or highlighting in the public space in entertaining media contents like movies or public commentary and presentation platforms like the on-air personalities.

These personalities, through a combination of social media, gossip/notoriety, and other appearances, are able to retain interest and followership, which they eventually are able to commercialize. These, according to Mark di Somma, had led to a business model that resulted in appearances in ads, licensing, endorsements, brand ambassador roles, private label brands, product lines, etc.

Product brands, according to Mark di Somma are the endpoint in the process of elevating the perceptions of commodities/goods such that they are associated with ideas and emotions that exceed their functional capability—a position where the summation of the individual parts is greater than the output of the individual parts separately.

Kali Hawlk pointed out that product branding gives the items in your portfolio an identity within the marketplace and allows them to stand out against what competitors are offering, creates an emotional connection for the customer and your product, and engenders brand loyalty that pulls customers into your product portfolio.

Product brands are also about the promise you make to your customers and how you deliver on that, and more especially the expectations you create in your customer through different elements of your product and how you meet or live up to such expectations. That is why a product can be positioned, transformed, or built up to have a larger-than-life attitude through adept product branding. An example is Coca-Cola, which if you are drinking it, you are not just drinking a carbonated soft drink, but you are enjoying the Coke side of life.

Ingredient brands: these are largely product brands only that they are component brands, which add to the value of another brand, based on the value it brings or adds to the other brand. They add to the overall value proposition of the brand that they are incorporated into and always featured or highlighted as part or components of the brands that they are embedded in. A very good example is Intel chips, which are always advertised as a component of the brand that houses them. These ingredient brands market themselves to consumers as essential ingredients or components to look for and take into consideration when purchasing such products or brands. Their presence within the brands bolsters confidence and adds credibility to the brands and, as such, is an essential factor in the purchase decision. A reverse example is bread, which is usually marketed as bromate free.

Generic brands are a type of consumer product that lacks a widely recognized name or logo because it typically isn't advertised. They are usually identified by product characteristics and are usually less expensive than their brand-name counterparts due to their lack of promotion, which can inflate the cost of a good or service. They are usually characterized by very basic packaging and labels and are designed as substitutes for more expensive brand-name goods.

According to Mark Di Somma, they are the brands you become when you lose distinctiveness and can exist in three main forms. The first type that is specific to the healthcare industry alludes to those brands that have fallen out of patent protection and now face competition from a raft of same-ingredient imitators known as generics.

The second form of generic brands is the brands where the name has become ubiquitous and, in so doing, has passed into common language as a verb often representing the various other groups of products within the same industry—Google, Xerox, Sellotape, etc. The third form is the unbranded, unlabelled product that has a functional description for a name but no brand value at all and represents the ultimate point in commoditization.

Challenger brands: a challenger brand is a brand in an industry where it is neither the market leader nor a niche brand. Challenger brands are categorized by a mindset that continuously challenges the status quo. They have business ambitions beyond conventional resources and are prepared to do something bold, usually against the existing conventions or codes of the category, to break-through. It is "less about business enmity, and more about an often mission-driven desire to progress the category in some way in the customer's favor."

They are also different from the disruptor brands, which are more focused on overtaking or becoming the market leader through a new or unique product offering. Challenger brands, according to the Challenger Project, are more often focused on *what* they are challenging (about the category drivers or the customer experience, for instance) than *who* they are challenging.

Challenger brands, according to the Challenger Project, are about breaking free from the habits and baggage that time wields, and instead looking, and continuing to look, at the category with fresh eyes; challenging a broader convention or dimension of their category, enabling them to completely redefine their industry, and how it's experienced. Interestingly challenger brands can either be product or corporate brands.

Luxury brands generally include goods for which their demand increases more than proportionally as income rises, such that expenditures on the good become a greater proportion of overall spending. They are in contrast to necessity goods, where demand increases proportionally less than income. The demand for luxury goods is, therefore, an elastic demand, meaning that consumers will spend more on luxury items once their income grows and, inversely, drops sharply when income declines.

A luxury brand is a brand that designs, produces, and sells high-end goods and services. A high-end brand is a brand that produces high-quality products with premium materials and craftsmanship expertise. The value of the products is, of course, subjective and usually the outcome of expert branding and marketing activities.

These high-end or prestige brands deliver social status and endorsement to the consumers. The positioning of these brands is usually between the borderline of exclusivity and reality or fantasy. They achieve this positioning through quality, association, and a compelling story, having perfected the delivery of image and aspiration to their markets.

A cult brand refers to a product or service that has a relatively small but loyal customer base that verges on fanaticism. It is usually a symbol-intensive brand that is tied to a single customer segment or a specific product category. A cult brand, unlike more traditional brands, has customers who feel a sense of self-ownership or vested interest in the brand's popularity and success.

The brands have been able to achieve a unique connection with the customers and are able to create a consumer culture that people want to be a part of. This they do by speaking or appealing to the customer's identity, ideology, or cultural milieu. The brand symbolizes a specific lifestyle and usually becomes more of an identity for the community which buying such a product enables them to fit in or identify with.

The relationship between the brand and its cult followers is a mixture of both love and madness or frenzy. These brands tend to be distinctive and provide an alternative style or feeling, which differs from existing brands, thereby helping the people differentiate them.

A good example of some brands that have attained cult status is the Harley Davidson motorcycle that people are willing to pay for and wait for upwards of a year or more to own one. Others are Mini Cooper, VANS, Apple, which people can line up and wait for upwards of a week or more to get the newly introduced products, etc.

A private brand is a good that is exclusively manufactured for and sold under the name of a specific retailer that is competing with other brand-name products within the same category. It can also be referred to as "private label" or "store brands" their prices tend to be less than those of nationally recognized name brand goods and usually provide retailers, such as supermarkets, with a better margin than the brand-name goods they also carry.

Private branded goods are usually made by third-party or contract manufacturers, often on the same production lines as other brands, with the only difference being the labels of the goods. This is a cost-effective way of producing a product without investment into large manufacturing facilities, designers, quality assurance personnel, or a specialized supply chain. This means of using outside manufacturing makes it possible for a retailer to offer a wide range of private-label goods that appeal to both cost-conscious shoppers as well as premium-product consumers. Nike, Apple, Zara, H&M are all private brands, as they do not own their own manufacturing facilities but are manufactured by third parties for them.

Clean slate brands are brands without heritage and history that have been able to connect with their consumers while capitalizing on the lust or craving for the new, instant trust, and open operation. Consumers are now attracted to unproven and unknown brands the way they were attracted to established brands in the past. In fact, 'established' is now often just another word for tired, old-fashioned if not tainted.

This lust for the new arises as a result of the new innovations in technology that have broken down the barrier of entry into several markets coupled with the launch of new, nimble, and more exciting products and services that are laser-focused on what the customer wants now as opposed to yesterday.

The instant trust also emanates from the loss of trust by the consumers in big businesses, especially in mature economies, such that new start-ups with exciting products are usually embraced as a better-preferred option. Good examples are Jumia, Uber, Bolt, and a lot of the other technology-driven companies that are taking over the market.

They are also successful and accepted because they come with no baggage of ethical and social malpractice coupled with their simple, lean operations.

Service Brands, as opposed to product brands, focus on the intangibles or the immaterial performances, which cannot be seen or touched, or their quality determined or assessed in advance before purchase or consumption. This makes the inherent risk in the service brands higher.

The variability in the quality of services is also due to the human element involved in the service delivery as the knowledge, competence, expertise, or attitude of the various customer service people are not the same.

Services are also produced and consumed simultaneously in space and/or time when the customer is involved and, as such, cannot be stored, exchanged, or returned, unlike a product.

According to deChernatony and Dall'Olmo Riley, the distinguishing factor between product and service branding lies in the executional strategy. Service brands depend on the culture of the organization and the training and attitudes of their employee, which is more difficult to build and sustain but is thankfully more difficult to copy.

The critical factors in service branding are the need for responsiveness in front-line staff; the mechanisms, such as empowerment, by which such responsiveness may be attained, good internal communication programs that enable greater consistency in the delivery of the customer service experience regardless of the customer's contact point within the organization.

This reverse hierarchy where all the organization's systems and processes are geared toward providing support for the customer service officers to facilitate the service delivery process is what differentiates the service brands from the product brand.

Public brands: according to Corinne Rochette, the public brand is a relative newcomer to the public sphere and is an expression of public marketing and an outcome of New Public Management (NPM). It is a lever that allows public organizations or government agencies to get across their identity, assert their legitimacy and provide markers for the evaluation of their actions.

Owing to the growing competition, the legitimacy crisis, fiscal pressures, technological revolutions (e-governance) that has changed the relationship with the public institutions and their user-clients and staff while transforming the place and operation of public organizations, the brand, though under-exploited, has become a very important lever to restore legibility and legitimacy to public organizations. It can also help them assert their difference, express their skills and mobilize its officials and employees toward the achievement of its objectives. It also has the potentiality of combining traditional values and approaches with new practices dictated by performance requirements.

Some experts like Mark Di Somma have also argued that the branding of an entity where there is a lack of consumer choice and a competitive model attached to it is a misnomer. However, there is a consensus that all organizations, regardless of their nature, inclusive of government agencies, can benefit from the disciplines and methodologies of brand strategy to add to stakeholders' understanding and trust of their entities.

Ethical brands can both be product or corporate brands and refer specifically to the mental or philosophical underpinnings that guide the operations of the brand, how it does business, the areas it operates, and also the kind of businesses that it engages in.

In other words, the ethical brand describes how brands work, specifically the practices they use and the commitments they demonstrate in areas such as worker safety, CSR, as well as a reassurance of responsible behavior by the brand, etc. A good example is the dropping of Chaokoh coconut milk by Costco and Target from the products they carry due to the allegation of forced monkey labor in harvesting the coconuts or the incidence of so many diamond sellers advertising themselves as not patronizing, dealing, or selling blood diamonds (diamonds from war-torn areas).

Place brands: this refers to a group of brands whose branding strategies are anchored on territorial or geographical location. Places in different locations across the globe are unique, very complex, and alive with their own uniqueness and peculiarities.

Territorial or place brands, according to Adam Mikolajczyk, have been described as reminiscent of the archaeologist's work, who rediscovers the DNA and history of the place and characteristically weaves or ties it to the future as well as the dreams and admirations of the contemporary people and less the work of a creator.

The peculiarity and challenge of place branding are that the branded core of a given place should be shaped or presented in such a manner that it does not lose its credibility in its bid to gain competitiveness and attention.

The peculiarity of the place that is being marketed should be aspirational and weaved toward the future even though it drives its credibility and authenticity from its history. A good example is the Rainbow Nation—South Africa, whose branding derives its credence from its history and cannot lay claim to any credibility if not for its history. However, the concept has so beautifully been weaved into what a beautiful future and potential the diversity of its colors can represent for the nation.

This challenge of finding such a subtle balance between the historical identity and this aspirational-competitive one is extremely difficult, but it is also at the nexus of the brand's potential and its infinite possibilities.

Nation brands, though quite different from national brands (the brand of a product that is distributed nationally under a brand name—owned by a producer or distributor—as opposed to local brands), are an extension of place branding. It seeks to measure, build and manage the reputation of countries and, according to Pauline Kerr, is "the application of corporate marketing concepts and techniques to countries, in the interests of enhancing their reputation in international relations.

Some of the main objectives of nation branding, according to Hwajung Kim, has been to remold national identities, enhance the nation's competitiveness, embrace political, cultural, business, and sports activities, promote economic and political interests at home and abroad, and alter, improve or enhance a nation's image/reputation.

Interestingly, Simon Anholt, the proponent of the concept of nation branding, believes that it is pernicious to believe that a country can simply advertise its way into a better reputation. For him, if a country is serious about enhancing its international image, it should simply concentrate on product development and marketing rather than chase after the cinema of branding.

At the end of the day, the question remains what advertises a nation or best builds its brand? The nation's advertising, its performances, and results in the global marketplace? Or is it its people and all exports from the country? For instance, what has best marketed India to the world? Is it the bevy of experts and computer whiz kids that it has exported to Silicon Valley and other blue-chip companies across the world? Bollywood or the government messages about India?

Global brands are recognized throughout much of the world, and firms employing this unified approach use a similar marketing strategy to support the brand and its development everywhere. This approach ensures consistency in presenting the brand's values in all of its markets.

The advantage of a global brand is that the firm can gain from marketing economies of scale. For example, the same advertising strategy can be employed worldwide using the same celebrities, words, and images. With the massive global growth and development of the internet, presenting a unified image through a standardized brand has become increasingly popular.

Successful global brands focus on presenting a unique, meaningful, and enduring image to their target market, which can be adapted to local demands. Maintaining a consistent global approach allows consumers to find and understand the brand wherever they are and creates global brand loyalty.

Denise Lee Yohn, however, in his treatise, argues that there are only nine different types of brands bearing in mind the strategic direction or stance that can be adopted in shaping the identity of the brand and positioning it. This, for him, is a simple shortcut for the brand manager or owner in determining the kind of brand that he wants to build.

For him, the nine types of brands are:

Disruptive brands which challenge the current ways of doing things and introduces new concepts that substantively change the market.

Conscious brands on a mission to make a positive social or environmental impact or enhance people's quality of life.

Service brands that consistently deliver high-quality customer care and service.

Innovative brands that consistently introduce advanced and breakthrough products and technologies.

Value brands that offer lower prices for basic quality.

Performance brands offer products that deliver superior performance and dependability.

Luxury brands offer higher quality at a higher price.

Style brands are differentiated through the way their products or services look and feel, as much as or more than by what they do.

Experience brands are differentiated through the experiences they provide, as much as or more than by the products or services themselves.

At the end of the day, the classifications of brands into different brand types and categories are left to the individual's preference or choice. For example, employer brands, NGOs, and non-profit brands, investor brands, activist brands can all be classified as different variations of the corporate or institutional brands but with different emphasis or focus. For instance, a single brand might be able to fit into all these differentiations on a large or small scale.

Activist brands, ethical brands, and challenger brands can also be classified as a mindset or as a business strategy adopted by different corporate brands in the pursuit of their business.

Ingredient brands can also be classified as part of the product brand, while celebrity brands are definitely part of personal brands.

CHAPTER FOUR

Why Some Brands Fail and Others Succeed—Brand Identity

Every year Interbrand publishes something like the Fortune 500 list of millionaires and billionaires for brands. In it, the top brands and their net worth are showcased. Interestingly some brands like Coca-Cola etc., have been regular features on the Interbrand list of global brands consecutively for the last ten years, whereas others have just shown a meteoric appearance and disappeared.

A good example is Nokia, which was worth $29.4b and number eight on the Interbrand list of global brands in 2010, Marlboro was number eighteen with a worth of $19.6b, Dell Computers number forty-one with a worth of $8.8b, Blackberry number fifty-four with a worth of $6.7b in 2010, but by 2019 all had disappeared from the list.

The question, therefore, arises why some brands are so successful in their brand marketing whereas others have never lived up to their bidding and many others just qualified as "also-ran" brands.

The success and failure rate for brands become very interesting if new products or brands are included in the equation. According to Nielsen statistics, more than 85 percent of new (Consumer

Packaged Goods) products fail, 95 percent of new products introduced each year fail. Up to 80 percent of new product launches in the consumer-packaged goods industry fail.

To put it in a better perspective, according to Harvard Business School Professor Clayton Christensen, each year, more than 30,000 new consumer products are launched, and between 80–95 percent of them fail.

What a horrific statistic, you will say. The extent of these product failures can only be imagined if the entire production and marketing cost of these 28,500 product failures are quantified in terms of the costs incurred, the man-hours and labor invested in these product failures, as well as the level of indebtedness in terms of bad loans that they create.

According to Joan Schnieder and Julie Hall, "The biggest problem or cause of these product failures is lack of preparation: Companies are so focused on designing and manufacturing new products that they postpone the hard work of getting ready to market them until too late in the game."

What then can be classified as this lack of preparation or preparations in the wrong areas, which have been responsible for brand and product failures? For clarification purposes, product or brand failure in this context can be defined as; the inability of a product to realize the required market share to sustain its presence in the market; or the ultimate failure of a product to achieve profitability.

We will not, at this point, delve into the product-brand continuum or definition but will stick basically to the brand perspective, the product-brand continuum we have already discussed earlier.

Brands fail due to so many reasons, which we will try to enumerate and elucidate on.

One of the major reasons why brands fail is as a result of a poor or ill-defined identity. Just like anyone who does not know who he or she is, their capacities (strengths or weaknesses) or what their sense of purpose or direction in life is will most likely not make any huge success or mark in life, so also will a brand that does not have a well-defined identity, a sense of purpose, etc. The same can also be said of a man who is bedeviled with an inferiority complex.

According to Jean Kapferer, a prominent brand authority, a brand is not the name of a product. It is the vision that drives the creation of products and services under that name. This vision, the key belief of the brand and its core values, is part of what is known as the brand identity. What, for instance, was the vision of BMW in producing all the cars within their brand portfolio? BMW will immediately tell you that what they had in mind in producing their cars was to produce "an ultimate driving machine," not just a car.

That mindset and awareness will underline and determine all the activities that go into the making of their cars, both in the quality, safety, reliability, and performance of all the parts and the technology involved. It also sets a benchmark for the brand in all its operations and activities.

The brand identity specifies the facets of the brands' uniqueness and value. In other words, why and how different or unique is your brand within the galaxies of other brands that seek to provide the same services or achieve the same goal as your own brand? For example, what is the unique thing or difference between Accenture Consulting and McKinsey, Deloitte, PWC, and other global consulting firms? What do they stand for, and why will you choose one of these consulting firms above the other? What are their value systems, strengths, specialties, and core competencies, and how does that resonate with you or your firm or the services for which you seek from them?

If a brand fails to present itself along these lines, then the point of differentiation will be blurred, and there will be no clearly remarkable lines or basis for choosing between the two brands. For every brand that has made a success in the market, there are very clear lines of demarcation between it and its competitors, which also serves as a basis of choice or preference. This can be said of Coca-Cola and Pepsi Cola, which despite the fact that in over 60 percent of blind taste experiments, people will prefer Pepsi Cola to Coca-Cola but the reaction to the bottled or branded contents are completely different with Coca-Cola leading the way.

In the vehicle category, Mercedes Benz cannot be mistaken or misconstrued for BMW and vice versa or Toyota for Lexus simply because each of these brands has been able to correctly identify itself and give value or life to all the products bearing their name. Hence in the Nigerian advertising parlance, "If it is not Panadol, it cannot be as good as Panadol" One who wants to buy a Mercedes Benz, BMW, or other car is very clear in his or her mind why he or she wants to buy the specific brand of the vehicle that he is purchasing. Especially as the brand these days accentuates the personality of the persons using them.

The clothing brands are also the same. A Gucci brand is completely different from a Louis Vuitton brand, same for a Raph Lauren, Lacoste, or a Tom Hilfiger brand. Although both brands are looked upon as iconic and legendary brands across the globe, Louis Vuitton, for example, is the more established of the brands and offers bags that have a timeless chic, elegant and sophisticated design that often has a high resale value. It is known for its respect for traditions and heritage and is usually for conservative people.

Gucci, on the other hand, focuses on innovations, creativity, a modern approach to fashion, is more edgy and courageous with the absence of stereotypes. Its focus is on how modern fashionistas should dress and is supported by dynamic young people who use the brand to highlight their individuality.

To succeed, therefore, as a brand, you must have a very clear definition of the identity of your brand, or else failure or an "also-ran" or a "me too brand" is in the offing.

What Is Brand Identity, and How to Build One

According to Kapferer, brand identity can be looked upon as an Identity card—a personal non—transferable document that tells in a few words who we are, what our name is, and what distinguishable features we have that can be instantly recognized. While this encompasses the logo, graphics, and other corporate function materials, it definitely goes beyond it. For example, the logo alone does not tell the customers who the brand is or what it stands for or the various factors that differentiate the brand from other competing brands within the same category. Some other things beyond the company logo tell the customers what the brand stands for.

One of the major reasons why brands fail is as a result of a poor or ill-defined identity. Just like anyone who does not know who he or she is, their capacities (strengths or weakness) or what their sense of purpose or direction in life is will most likely not make any huge success or mark in life, so also will a brand that does not have a well-defined identity, sense of purpose, etcetera.

For example, as differentiating as the logo of UNN and UI is or Harvard and Yale or Stanford; it is not the logo alone that tells the teeming populates about the ideological and philosophical differences that define or determine the differences in approach both in teaching, admissions, areas of emphasis or research between the various universities. Certain approaches that are admissible or acceptable to one university, though right, may not be acceptable to the other university. Regardless of these, the logo and company graphics is a good place to commence the real identity creation process for the brand. In doing that, you do well to ask or go beyond the logo aesthetics, beauty, or harmony to what differentiating characteristics in terms of the brand's core the logo communicates to the customers?

Brand identity also refers to an identity of opinion, an identical point of view, or the common element that sends a single message amidst the variety of its products, actions, and communications. This is similar to a unique voice or shade of opinion that is peculiar and attributable to the brand or its products. If you are a car or vehicle, what is your opinion about cars? For example, Microsoft operated and built a multi-billion industry based on the simple principle of democratizing computer technology. They believed that computers should be made available to everyone hence the deviation from the workstations and big computers of their time. Apple also built its brand on the principle of producing an easy-to-use, user-friendly computer. Dell computers did the same, also.

Your perspective, view, opinion, or point of view about the industry that you are operating in is what determines the identity of your brand, your *raison d' etre*, or your reason for being. Your understanding of the need, essence, or niche in which you want to operate or what created the need of your business in the first instance is the basic ingredient for the building of your brand identity. If you do not have a clear sense of the need or space in the market that you want to serve or fill, then you are virtually an also-ran business and cannot have a distinguishing sense of identity on which to build the brand.

Brand identity refers to the features of the brand, which despite the various changes in physical appearance or civil status, still remains the same and unchanged like the fingerprints. Brand identity encapsulates how time will or can change the unique and permanent quality of the sender, brand, or retailer without detracting from its very essence or core values or personae. This is why a 1990 Ferrari, though radically different from the present design of Ferrari, bears or encapsulates the indelible signature and essence of the brand that is completely unmistakable to any of the car's customers. The same applies to the various design changes of Mercedes 230 over the years. Despite the changes in the design, the unmistakable signature and imprint or identity of Mercedes remains very obvious and clear in all the brands. For some brands, the design changes are not only inconsistent but also incongruent with the previous designs, thereby creating a huge confusion in the minds of their customers in their bid to carry over the brand affiliations and sentiments from design changes or modifications to another. A good example of this is Citroen vehicles.

Another brand that has maintained this consistency in all their brand designs is Coca-Cola, which has successfully replicated the curvature design in all their designs, both for the bottle and for the plastics also.

Jean-Noel Kapferer drilled down these elements of the brand identity into six, which he then presented as "the brand identity prism." The key elements of the prism are physique, personality, culture, relationship, self-image, and reflection, which according to him, are the key ingredients required in the building of a strong brand identity/ brand. **Strong brands are capable of weaving all aspects [of the prism] into an effective whole in order to create a concise, clear, and appealing brand identity.**

The brand identity prism places these six elements in relation to each other by taking into consideration their position within the business, what the sender sees, has in his mind, what the client or recipient sees or experiences, and vice versa. The areas defined between these points range from what goes on internally within the organization (personality, culture, self-image) to what extends or reaches out to the external (physique, relationship, reflection) and the many paths that can be drawn to join each area.

BRAND IDENTITY PRISM

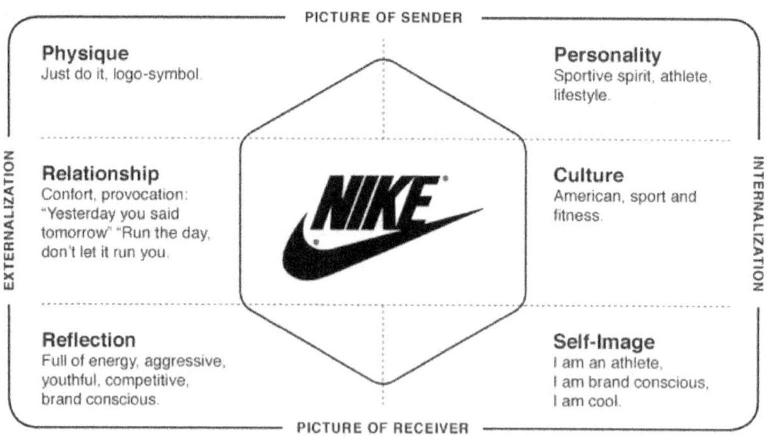

Using Nike, for instance, to explain Kapferer's brand identity prism

Physique

The physical characteristics of a brand refer to how we define the brand and how it will manifest, including its visual features—visual cues that help consumers identify the brand. So when you think about Nike, you imagine highly innovative, creative, state-of-the-art shoes for prime performance, comfort, and class.

Brand Identity refers to the features of the brand, which despite the various changes in physical appearance or civil status still remains the same and unchanged like the fingerprints.

Personality

The brand's personality or character refers to the traits of the brand in the eyes of the consumer. One way of understanding this concept would be to imagine your favorite brand as a living thing. What kind of living thing will it be? How will it behave? Nike will ordinarily be looked at as a person that knows no boundaries or limitations by breaking all possible frontiers. This was why Nike went a long way in designing a set of athletic shoes that would help Eliud Kipchoge, the Kenyan athlete, break the two-hour marathon world record in a widely televised event across the entire world.

Culture

This refers to the set of values that feed into or set a foundation for the brand. In some cases, this will include the culture and values of the brand's country of origin. In the case of Nike, it is the American dream of surmounting all impossibilities and rising from inherent disadvantages to become a hero.

Self- Image

Self-image relates to the way in which customers see themselves in a particular brand. Brands can use self-image to their advantage by incorporating it into their identities. Self-image is like a mirror the target group holds up to itself—by associating themselves with certain brands, they see themselves differently. Nike brands make the customers look cool, trendy, and athletic.

Reflection

Self-image and reflection, according to Caileigh Lombard, differ in a noteworthy way: self-image refers to the customers' ideas of themselves, whereas reflection refers to how a brand portrays its target audience. Reflection is a set of stereotypical beliefs or attributes of a brand's target market, which is often highlighted in ads and other communications. Nike makes its target audience look youthful, full of energy, competitive, trendy, and brand-conscious or discerning.

Relationships

This refers to the nature of the relationship between the brand and its consumers, like what specific services are offered. How a brand connects with its audience and the type of relationship, it wants to build with its consumers. A superlative example of this is Harley Davidson motorcycles, where the consumers on their own organize Harley Davidson rallies, road trips, etc.

In summary, embedded in the concept of the brand identity, according to Kapferer, is the brand's particular vision and aim; what makes it different; the need being fulfilled by the brand; the brand's permanent nature; its values or value, it's field of competence or legitimacy and the signs that make it recognizable. These issues, when comprehensively incorporated in the brand identity, form the brand charter, which will form the basis of managing the brand in the medium and long term. This charter then forms the basis of managing the brand both in terms of the form and content of the present and future communication as well as extension issues.

One can justifiably seek to know or find out the importance of this painstaking process in defining or building the brand's identity. The concept of brand identity allows a closer connection with reality, especially with the increased complexity of today's marketing problems. By the time you would have gone through the rigor of developing an identity for your brand, you would have succeeded in laying the groundwork for a foundation that will not only help you build your brand but also act as a check for all your creative and communication people to avoid deviation from the brand essence in your creative developments and communication. Without a very clear brand identity, you would have surrendered the brand development to the vagaries of intuition and creative bursts that will vary from one creative director or communication person to another, thereby leading to conflicts and confusion among your customers.

Brand competition and the intense pressure to keep up with brand innovations within the industry is also another important reason why a clear brand identity is essential. The development of the ABS in cars is one example. In adopting this technological device in a car, a car driven by safety as an essential ingredient in its brand identity like Volvo cannot use it in the same way as a car like Mercedes or BMW that prides itself in powerful performance. The same applies to the current aerodynamic style of car building in the different kinds of cars. A car without a clear brand identity in trying to adopt all these developments will get muddled up and lose every sense of its identity in the marketplace. With a loss of this identity or differentiation in the marketplace, the brand loses its attractiveness and consequently market share, as customers will not patronize a brand that does not have anything to offer it in terms of enhancing their own individuality or personality.

Without a clear brand identity, it will also be impossible to position the brand in the minds of the consumers since positioning refers to the process of emphasizing and highlighting the distinctive characteristics of the brand that make it different from its competitors.

CHAPTER FIVE

Why Some Brands Fail and Others Succeed—Other Factors

Brand Authenticity, Originality, and Believability

Another set of factors that are contributory to the success and failures of brands are their authenticity, believability, and originality. In a nutshell, how credible and believable are your brand propositions, claims, and positions?

For instance, is there any real positive correlation between the usage of Nike products and actual extraordinary performance in sports? If you are not a superstar or a high-performing athlete, will the usage of Nike products suddenly boost or enhance your ability to perform or deliver results in your chosen field of sports? Will you suddenly obtain or acquire some superpower abilities to perform simply by the utilization of these sports wears? I guess we all know the answers.

The real issue is, therefore, how Nike has been able to own and be associated with superlative and extremely successful performance in the field of sports such that a lot of people will suddenly feel good, distinguished, or classy by adorning any one of their sports wears in the field of play? This feat was definitely not an accident but was achieved through a deliberate process of building their brand, associating it with and sponsorship of superstars who repeatedly endorse and wear their brands such that the superlative performance of these sportsmen and women gets transferred and positively associated with the clothes that they wear.

Nike, over the years, perfected the art of sponsorships and endorsements to the point that unique Nike sub-brands were created for these extremely successful sportsmen and women. Ranging from Jordan to Federer (before now) to Nadal, with each of them having specially designed custom-made shoes and clothing lines branded for them, which were later sold in the market at great profit. In the words of the popular advert, "Everyone wants to be a Tiger."

The flip side of this is also the "one hundred disease killer drug"—"gbogbomishe," which are prominently being peddled in Lagos molue buses and at other locations for a nominal amount of money. These drugs are presented as cures to all imaginable diseases—headache, back pain, fever, malaria, dysentery, etc. At the end of the day, which one of these propositions as to what the drug cures are actually believed and trusted by the customers?

Believability, therefore, refers to the quality of being credible, convincing, or realistic. In making claims for your brands, the first thing to ask or find out is how credible these claims are. In other words, to be credible, there must have been an antecedent of performance or history or background of validated or proven performance. Claims no matter how beautiful, poetic or pleasant to the ears CANNOT stand alone. They must be resting or dependent on a proven foundation of performance or proof.

The second question to ask is, who will or how do you intend to provide this background or history of performance. The credibility, integrity, and personality or weight of the source on which you want to depend on providing this attestation are key.

The source, style, or format of providing this testimony is also dependent on the industry or sector in which you operate and what the appealing, interesting, or credible authorities in those areas are. For instance, the surgeon general is a venerated authority or reference point for all issues of health, similarly to the Dental Council for issues that have to do with dentistry.

Every field has a set of credible or reference sources, which are continuously being looked up to, and their statements or words are like holy grails in those areas. For instance, if you are a lover of the Grand Prix, any claim or statement by Michael Schumacher will be regarded as incontrovertible because he has proven to be a huge success with so many laurels in his racing career. Every field or sector has its own version of Michael Schumacher, and any endorsement by them will put paid to any controversy about the quality claims of such brand offerings. Anthony Joshua, for instance, is an ambassador for Range Rover for a reason, mainly because Range Rover wants to associate itself with the high-octane performance of Anthony Joshua.

A credible source in one area can also be transferable to other areas or segments of the market. Due to the high speed, efficiency, and high performance of the Grand Prix, Michael Schumacher can be an accepted source of credibility for high and exceptional performance across other industries where such features are key, which is the reason why high performing vehicle brands such as Mercedes Benz use such credible individuals in advertising their cars.

The challenge, therefore, is to find the most credible sources that appeal or connect with your customer base and to build your brand claims, and to offer through the instrumentality of those sources, statistics, and facts such that the claims of your brand can become more credible or believable. Any effort to build your brand claim on shadows as opposed to substance will definitely lead to brand failures.

You will also need to ascertain the authenticity of these claims. A brand claim can be believable but not authentic. Authenticity simply means acting in ways that are consistent or show your true self and how you feel or expressing your whole self genuinely without any element of make-believe, forming or falsehood, or trying to be who you are not. To succeed in being authentic, you first have to know who your true self actually is.

A good example of a lack of authenticity is Hyundai Genesys and Equus. Hyundai, a low-cost, low-budget brand, turns around to position one of its brands within the luxurious sector of the market. If one wanted a luxurious brand, he would not go for Hyundai in the first place. Several luxurious brands exist that can meet that need better than Hyundai Genesys or Equus.

Volvo as a brand cannot also position itself on the basis of speed. The key essence of Volvo is safety, and so speed cannot be compatible at the same time with Volvo's brand essence, but for a brand like Mercedes Benz or BMW that prides itself in very high performance, speed will be a very credible and authentic part of their claims.

To be authentic, therefore, the brand has to be true to itself in all its claims and its propositions. If the brand is not clear about who it is or what it stands for, it will bring up a lot of confusing and inauthentic claims and positions. This will create a lot of disconcerting views and dispositions in the minds of the customers such that they will be confused as to what the brand really stands for, thereby abandoning it, which will lead to a huge failure for the brand.

A third dimension of the brand's proposition that can lead to a failure or success for the brand is its originality. Authenticity means being real or true to yourself, whereas originality refers to being the first person to make such claims or propositions. Originality also means being one of a kind or having existed in the same form from the beginning. Being original also means that you are not a copycat and that, in actual fact, there is no other brand like you in the market. It also alludes to your difference and irreplaceability in the marketplace. You are evolving or developing along your own chosen lines of progress and not trying to be another brand or be like another brand. Rather you are being true to yourself.

Coca-Cola and Pepsi Cola, despite being carbonated drinks, have pursued several different and original pathways to the development of their brands. Coca-Cola came out with claims and propositions of being the real thing; Coca-Cola is it. Pepsi Cola, on the other hand, came out with propositions as refreshing and invigorating, a fine bracer before a race; why take less when Pepsi is the best; more bounce to the ounce and then the Pepsi generation, the choice for a new generation, and a generation ahead.

The key factor was that none sought to copy or imitate the other. Differentiation along your originally chosen direction is the key to developing a brand. When you lose sight of your originality or what actually differentiates or makes you different, you will lose the essence of your brand and will subsequently fail as a brand.

Brand clarity
Brand clarity or lack of it is another reason why brands succeed or fail. Brand clarity, according to Hanafi Sam, is how your brand

works in general and talks about every small detail of your brand, including your design and brand experience.

Clarity or lucidity refers to a perception or understanding that is free or devoid of indistinctness or ambiguity, the state or quality of being clear or transparent to the eye. When people talk or refer to your brand, what do they actually mean or imply? Communication by its very nature can be understood or interpreted differently depending on the various individuals and their different peculiarities. Regardless of that, the clarity of your messaging or perception by your customers and consumers will preclude a lot of options that are undesirable or unintended by the brand owner. It reduces the extent of confusion and ambiguity about the brand because it is clearly defined and explained in terms of its purpose etc.

Clarity in terms of your messaging and purpose presupposes a clear and unambiguous understanding of who your brand is, what it wants to be or grow into, as well as a clear understanding of your audience, their nuances, cultures, beliefs, style of communication, and relationships. If you do not understand who you are or what you are trying to become, or who your audience is, then you will definitely be driving or piloting your communication toward an undesirable or unintended direction that will not be impactful or useful to both parties, especially to the brand. This is usually why there is oftentimes a disconnect between what the brand is trying to communicate about itself and what the people are perceiving and understanding, which could be distasteful or disconcerting for both parties.

If your brand is a person, clarity will refer to the people who you are trying to describe or explain your brand to being able to understand and develop a clear picture or perception of who the brand is, what it will likely do, or how it will behave in different situations or contexts; who its associates will be and the kinds of ideas or position that it will advocate, propose or support.

Clarity is important because simplicity not only empowers the communicator but also frees the recipient from errors of meaning due to lack of clarity. Complexity in content and message strangle good communications and will often leave your audience lost in intent and making assumptions in purpose and desired outcomes. Simple and clear direction produces higher quality results.

Clarity also improves connection and engagement primarily because it increases trust and transparency. It exposes purpose by unveiling expectations and telling people exactly what you want. Clarity and concise messaging are also essential in convincing people both about your intent and to also take action.

Brand clarity encompasses all the vital elements about your brand; your brand strategy, brand story, brand essence, brand attributes/ values, brand personality, brand positioning, your target market, etc. The ability to identify the fundamental elements as well as the core of your brand is essential in achieving brand clarity.

It is important to emphasize the point that clarity exists at two points; that of the brand communicator and the brand consumers. The clarity or assumed clarity at the point of the brand communicator does not immediately or automatically translate into a sense of clarity for the consumers. However, the two points converge at a point because increased clarity at the point of the brand communicator will eventually lead to increased clarity for the consumers so long as the two are willing and constantly open in exchanging ideas and information.

Diageo is one brand that invests and shares its marketing clarity across its business. The brand makes its DWBB model (the Diageo Way of Brand Building) central to its marketing culture and internal communications because it forces clarity on those responsible for assets like Johnnie Walker, Smirnoff, Baileys, Guinness, etc.

The markets in which we operate are growing harder to understand, but brands that invest in clarity will out-perform those that run on the vapor of instinct.

Brand presence

Brand presence is another critical element in the success or failure of a brand. Presence refers to the fact of being in a particular place, the state of being present or someone or something that is seen or noticed in a particular place, area, etc.

Looking at presence purely from this perspective will lead to the proposition of a physical solution to the problem, like in the area of distribution where the presence of a brand or product is basically looked upon as an availability issue. The brand is present when the physical units of the brands are available in the store or shops and warehouses.

As valid as that perspective is, brand presence encompasses a lot more variables and ideas than that. Presence can also be etched in mind by all the various interactions and experiences the consumer or customer has had with the brand over time, such that even when the brand is not physically available, there is a longing or preference for the brand. In other words, the memory of the brand that is existing or resident in the mind is almost like a love affair, deal, or relationship. This is why customers will go into the store and ask for a particular brand and, if it is not available, will not be assuaged or convinced to buy a different one.

The third aspect of brand presence refers to the various physical or psychological cues or reminders about the brand that keeps alive the feelings and fondness about the brand in the minds of the customers/consumers. For example, Billboards, Coca-Cola paintings, and displays at the back of their truck. These aid brand recall.

The fourth aspect of brand presence is remarkability or reckon and attraction. A person, for instance, can be at a meeting or at a party and will just be noted as being present, whereas another person can be at the party and the cynosure of all attention and attraction. As a matter of fact, the person will be the toast of all attention and the life of the party. The first person is present or available at the party, whereas the second person has a presence.

The same analogy can be attributed to brands in the marketplace. Some brands are just present in the market place whereas others have a presence and are the toast of the marketplace. Other brands don't get to be sold or noticed until the other brands have finished selling or had their day in the marketplace. Presence here refers to a larger-than-life attribute endowed upon the brand such that oftentimes even what the brand does not claim to do can be attributed to the brand. Guinness has run a couple of verygood adverts in Nigeria that led to an increased presence of the brand. One of such was Udeme, my friend and Black thing good oooo!! These all utilized regular parlance and innuendos in the country.

A brand that focuses mainly on the first parameter of presence without first cultivating the second and third parameters is mainly applying a push strategy and may run into a situation where the brands fully flood the stores without a pull strategy that will facilitate a pull through the stores.

Presence is, therefore, more of a mental construct akin to the child who, despite his father not being around, is well aware of what the father wants and will not want to go against him or offend the father despite his absence. That is also why parenting based on fear or physical monitoring as opposed to self-monitoring is usually not very successful.

According to InterBrand, presence measures the degree to which a brand feels omnipresent and how positively consumers, customers, and opinion formers discuss it in both traditional and social media.

Brand presence is, therefore, about establishing your brand in the lives of your consumers. This is a 360-degree approach to branding that makes your brand an essential aspect of every area of your consumer's life. A good example of such an approach was the advert run by Coca-Cola (Coca-Cola moments), where the different occasions where consumers can take or drink Coke alongside their other foods and other activities were highlighted. Similar advert executions were adopted by Peak milk.

> *A brand with a huge brand presence will always be a winner in the market place whereas one which has not been able to break through the clutter and establish itself will always be a misnomer and a failure or at best an also ran brand.*

A company with a solid brand presence has its content and services built into the very fabric of its market vertical such that the brand can be seen or viewed as a life enabler, an essential part of the lives of its customers and consumers, and not just as an external intruder. A good example is Kelloggs and what it has been able to achieve in positioning its brand as an essential aspect of the individual's life for every moment and type of cereal.

A brand with a huge brand presence will always be a winner in the market place whereas one which has not been able to break through the clutter and establish itself will always be a misnomer and a failure or, at best, an also-ran brand.

Another brand that has done this exceptionally well and scores high in presence is Starbucks, which has successfully established itself as the third place from home after the workplace. With its various flavors, most people cannot wait to have their next coffee fill or kick. This process of enduing life to a brand such that it does not only have relevance to the lives of the consumers but also becomes something that they can engage with is the sole essence of brand management.

Brand engagement
Brand engagement is another key parameter that determines the success or failure of brands. Brands can be seen as inanimate objects or can be made to have a life of their own. To engage with the brand, therefore, the brand must first of all have assumed a life of its own. Without such a life and personality of its own, people cannot engage with the brand.

A brand like Wimbledon has assumed a larger-than-life attitude on its own such that in some people's calendar, it is a must-attend event every year. Same for our teeming population that has developed avid followership of Premiership League such that life over any weekend without premiership soccer is like a death sentence. Bhurj Arab Hotel at a time had to organize an exhibition match for Roger Federer and Rafa Nadal to play a Lawn Tennis match on their helipad, which was turned into a full Lawn Tennis court just to create a platform of engagement.

Brand engagement is, therefore, the process of forming an emotional or rational attachment between a consumer and a brand. Consumers and customers are usually apathetic and indifferent about a brand, so brand engagement is the process of getting the customers out of their shells or points of apathy to becoming mentally, physically, and emotionally involved with your brand.

The brand adoption continuum among consumers generally evolves from the stage of lack of awareness to the point of rejection or brand advocacy or becoming a brand ambassador.

Brand engagement exists basically at two levels; one at the level of the employees and internal stakeholders and the other at the point of the external stakeholders and customers/consumers.

To successfully engage your staff and internal stakeholders, the key is in ensuring that the entire promise of the image created in the minds of the employees—the employee brand is delivered on the joining of the employees. If the promise made is not kept, it will lead to dissatisfaction, disaffection, lack of trust, and employee turnover. You cannot expect employees who are not satisfied with the brand to be advocates of the brand and not to de-market or bad-mouth the brand.

This is so important because your employees are the main interface of the brand with the external stakeholders and customers/consumers. If they do not believe or strongly advocate for the brand and are passionate about the brand, you cannot expect the customers and consumers who interface with them to be passionate or actively engaged with your brand.

To build your brand engagement platform, you also need to ensure that employees and close stakeholders of an organization completely understand the organization's brand and what it stands for. This will ensure that their activities on a day-to-day basis are contributing toward expressing that brand through the customer experience they create or facilitate for the customer. The story of the Ritz-Carlton Hotel in Singapore that had to fly one of their employees to Bali to pick up a particular kind of an egg from a specialty store due to the allergy of their guest, a distance of 1676 Km or two-hour-and-forty-minute flight is a good example of engaged/committed employees creating wonderful customer service experience for their customers.

The second aspect of brand engagement is the customers/consumers and other external stakeholders. Brand engagement, like we said earlier, represents a relationship between a brand and its consumers, and that relationship is driven by interactions.

Marshal Carper outlined seven levels of brand engagement; *consuming content, making small shows of support, participating in conversations, championing the brand, being physically present, and creating brand content. The seventh level, buying a product, is a given as one cannot go through the outlined levels without buying or patronizing the product.*

A very good example of top-notch brand engagement is Harley Davidson, where the fans have their own fan page, organize regular events, and even have regular roadshows on their own. People are prepared to pay and wait for months for the brand to be delivered to them.

Brand engagement is built on conversations and activities, so if your brand is not talking or engaging your customers in a conversation, then it is failing in its main responsibilities of engaging its customers and consumers. Higher levels of engagement are synonymous or correlate with increases in revenue.

Another essential ingredient in the success or failure of a brand is its **consistency** or lack of it. Consistency means the steadfast adherence to the same principles, course, form, etc. (Every action/activity has a thought process or firm belief system behind them, so you are only consistent when there is seamless continuity in that thought process that underlines your activities) So if the principle behind your actions is to be the best you cannot at a different point start cutting corners just because there are pressures or difficulties in the environment. A good example of this is Toyota in their "Good thinking, good product"—Yoshida advertisement.

It refers to agreement, harmony, or compatibility, especially correspondence or uniformity among the parts of a complex thing. The confusion about consistency is the erroneous impression that it is opposed to dynamism, adaptation or that consistency is inflexible and unwavering as well as opposed to change.

Consistency first identifies the core and essential elements of the brand, the brand essence that cannot change without altering the DNA of the brand. Once these core elements are identified, the peripherals or outer part of the brand, which are not so germane in defining the personality of the brand, will also be identified. The brand cannot compromise or afford to be inconsistent with its brand essence (what the brand stands for, is known, or wants to be known for). Else it will lose its meaning and value in the marketplace. For example, the brand logo and typography, fonts, etc., cannot be compromised because any atom of inconsistency in these and other key elements of the brand will lead to distrust and suspicion among the consumers or customers.

Brand consistency, therefore, is the practice of always delivering messages that are in line with the identity and values of your brand. Consistency here means that your target audience is being exposed to the same core messages repeatedly because the more consistent your messaging, the more consistent your branding.

Consistence in the core messaging is hugely important because over time and with consistent exposure, brands get associated with key elements and character traits just like an individual such that any deviation in such messaging will be inconsistent with the character traits and personae, thereby leading to confusion as to the true nature, behavior, and characteristics of the brands. Coca-Cola has consistently emphasized the same thing about themselves over the years in different ways and formats but still the same message. *Coca-Cola is it, Coca-Cola the real thing, Things go better with Coke, Always Coca-Cola, etc.*

Brands engender trust and are the true store of value and assets primarily because customers and consumers know what these brands stand for. Any deviation or inconsistency in what the true essence of these brands is will automatically break the trust and belief that the consumers have about the brand, thereby leading to a lack of patronage.

Brand consistency also leads to brand recognition, but if there are constant variations in the identity elements of the brand, then recognition will not be possible. It also evokes a positive emotion about your brand if positive single-minded messages are consistently communicated or passed across by your brand. This is why the proponents of advertising usually advocated for a single

Unique Selling proposition. On the whole, your brand consistency will help you stand out from the competition as your customers will definitely have something different or unique to associate or know your brand with.

A brand that is inconsistent in its messaging, purpose, or claim will definitely fail. Experience has shown that brands that jump from one advert execution-style, concept, messaging, or claim to another such that over time you cannot identify what the brand really stands for will definitely fail. Some of these brands do this to copy or try to counter claims by other brands without knowing that standing or sticking to one core messaging over the years will lead to a clear differentiation in the market. This is why it has been said that he who stands for nothing falls for everything.

Note that consistency in the core messaging does not mean that a single message must be adhered to and cannot be changed. Coca-Cola has changed its pay-off line like so many other brands over the years, but each of those messages is still consistent with the core essence of the brand. So the challenge, therefore, is in changing and growing but not deviating from your core essence as a brand.

Brand commitment
Brand commitment can be looked upon from two different perspectives; the commitment of the brand and its owners to the customers/consumers and the commitment of the customers/consumers to the brand.

Commitment is basically the state or quality of being dedicated to a cause, activity, engagement, or obligation that restricts freedom of action. Sung and Campbell, in their work, stated that commitment is the basic ingredient or variable that sustains a relationship between the customer/ consumer and the brand, same as trust without which there will be no relationship.

Commitment can therefore be defined as the enduring desire to maintain a valued relationship, with mutual commitment being the foundation of any meaningful relationship. Following from the definition above, brand commitment can therefore not be one-dimensional. Else it is no longer based on the relationship paradigm. The commitment must therefore be mutual from the brand to the customers/ consumers and from the customers/consumers to the brand with the brand, as a matter of fact, initiating or spearheading the relationship since the overall benefit from the relationship will be weighing more to the advantage of the brand and its owners.

Morgan and Hunt further posited that commitment and trust are 'key variables' in the exchange network between a company and its various partners because these variables encourage the company to invest in a long-term relationship. Marketing mix activities and brand management decisions, according to Fournier, can now be looked upon as 'behaviors' exhibited by the brand as part of this relationship continuum.

One model that has been successfully used over the years to define the concept of commitment is the Investment model, which in itself is based or predicated on three factors; satisfaction with the relationship, alternatives to the relationship, and investments in the relationship.

Brand Commitment, according to some marketing professionals, is, therefore, a comprehensive and flexible tool that very simply measures the psychological links between customers/users and the brand, product, or service, which allows us to estimate the possible brand potential and to predict the risk of leaving it to other brands.

Commitment is basically a psychological or mental state that showcases a state of dependence on a relationship, a long-term orientation toward it, feelings of attachment to a partner, and a desire to maintain the relationship. It shows us the amount of work/ investment required to maintain the relationship or to avoid other alternative relationships, as well as the risks or danger signs that may threaten or jeopardize such relationships, which we need to work very hard to avoid.

Most marketing professionals have confused brand commitment with brand loyalty; however, there is a thin distinction between the two concepts. Fournier defined brand commitment as an emotional or psychological attachment to a brand within a product class or as a long-term behavioral and attitudinal disposition toward a relational brand. In other words, brand loyalty is a behavioral concept, whereas brand commitment is an attitudinal concept. One can be behaving in a particular manner over time, either due to upbringing, conditioning, etc., without being personally convinced or mentally attuned to the rationale for such behaviors such that a change can always occur if the situations or circumstances necessitating such behaviors change. However, someone who is committed to a cause is mentally convinced as to why he or she is embarking on such behaviors such that regardless of the changes in the situation or circumstances, will still remain committed to the cause. Commitment is, therefore, both behavioral and attitudinal, whereas loyalty could only be behavioral. Some have, however, argued that true loyalty encompasses the element of commitment.

Beatty et al., in their studies, found out that the consumers' psychological attachment to a brand will be stronger if a brand provides them either hedonic or symbolic values. In other words, if brands provide superior benefits, which in turn results in satisfaction, consumers will commit themselves to establish, develop, and maintain a relationship with such brands.

Consequently, the brand, in trying to showcase its commitment to the consumers, has to invest in the customer/ consumer relationship so as to ensure the satisfaction of the buyers and ensure that they do not explore or deviate from forming other alternative relationships with other brands.

One-way brands have been able to achieve this objective has been through augmenting or adding additional value to the brand experience. Sponsorships and corporate responsibility programs have also been some other means of showcasing such commitment.

One calls to remembrance some years back when Guinness—Diageo embarked on a huge social responsibility/sponsorship program when it shot and premiered the Michael Power Film across the country in a blitzkrieg of marketing activities, promotions, etc. Such an event that goes beyond the simple marketing and showcasing the brand goes a very long way in demonstrating the brand's commitment to the customers/ consumers. Guilder Ultimate search is also another sterling example of a brand's commitment to itself and its relationship with its customers and consumers.

Customer/ consumer commitment to the brand is a much more straightforward thing like we pointed out and encompasses a psychological or mental state of dependence on the relationship or romance if you choose to stay with the brand; a long-term orientation toward it, feelings of attachment to the brand and a desire to maintain the relationship and not trade it with other brands.

Brand commitment is important because it reduces uncertainty and saves the consumer the cost of seeking new relational exchanges with alternative brands. Without a very strong commitment to the brand from both the brand side and the customers/consumers' side, the brand is very sure to die and not succeed. A half-hearted and nonchalant attitude toward the brand by its owners or employees is a sure recipe for failure and death.

Brand Responsiveness

Response is basically an act of responding or reacting to stimuli, either internal or external. Responsiveness could mean several different things depending on different scenarios. For instance, commercial responsiveness is the ability of a business to react quickly and appropriately in different situations, both in the selling and post-sale phases. Sales, "responsiveness" means that the company is delivering to the customer what is required as quickly as possible, whereas customer responsiveness measures the speed and quality at which your company provides customer service and communication. If a customer has to wait five days just for a simple email response, they might be more willing to take their business elsewhere. The central underlining factor in responsiveness is the speed of getting back to the customer on essential issues, observations, and complaints with regards to the brand, product, etc.

Lynda Decker, in her explanation of brand responsiveness, introduced the concept of an agile and adaptable branding approach that adjusts in alignment with a changing marketplace, thereby incorporating a lot more issues other than just speed.

Responsiveness is critical in brand marketing because it conveys more than most others concepts of marketing your level of regard, consideration, or value for the customer. Everybody, especially your customers who invest time and resources in your brand, wants to be treated with respect and be shown that they matter or are valued. Responsiveness is also one of the critical aspects of the service quality dimensions that are used in measuring customer satisfaction. Brand responsiveness, therefore, has a direct correlation ship with customer satisfaction.

Important elements of responsiveness are time, communication, information, and reaction to identified or highlighted issues. The quality of the brand responsiveness will be measured or evaluated based on these parameters. Brand responsiveness could involve the development of different augmenting factors to bolster the value and acceptance of the brand. It could also require some brand extension approaches to cover some integral aspects of the evolving market or the dissemination of important information that can assuage the customer's feelings, inform or clarify certain issues for them, etc.

Responsiveness could therefore imply doing something to the brand or to the customers and other external issues around the brand. Considering brand responsiveness, as reacting and responding to the customers and other externalities without an alteration or modification of certain aspects of the brand, may not be an accurate and complete explanation of the concept. A good example was when Coca-Cola, in its bid to respond to the increasing competitiveness of Pepsi Cola, introduced the new Coca-Cola formulation. They did not anticipate the huge backlash or push back from the consumers, which eventually made them return the original Coca-Cola formula as the Classic Coke.

Brand responsiveness is also unique because the vehicle through which the brand responds to its customers or consumers is the brand employees. Brand responsiveness, according to Parasuraman et al., involves the responsiveness of willing employees in telling customers exactly when things will be done, giving them undivided attention, promoting services, and responding in accordance with their requests. In other words, both organizational willingness and ability to help customers or respond to their needs, and to provide quick service with proper timelines as well as the willingness of employees to provide the required service at any time without any inconvenience are all essential aspects of brand responsiveness.

Pertinent questions to ask in trying to be responsive as a brand are do you know your customers/ audience (both primary and secondary), what are their perceptions about your brand (both positive and negative), what are their perceptions about competitive brands (both positive and negative), are there service issues associated with your brand through the distribution line and also at the customer service point? What are the key or prevalent trends in your chosen market?

In talking about distribution issues, what are the preferred packaging styles and sizes that will be more acceptable to your customers/ consumers, what price or value points are most acceptable to specific aspects or groups of your target market? A good example of an organization that exploited this very well to its advantage is Cowbell Milk. Cowbell Milk came into the market with its sachet milk based on an understanding of the customer—who may not have the money to buy a full tin of milk. These insights informed Cowbell Milk's strategy of coming up with the sachet milk, which was a big banger. It led to a huge market share gain for Cowbell such that all other milk companies, even Peak Milk, which was hitherto only positioning itself along the lines of quality, started producing their milk in sachets so as to avoid a huge erosion in their market share. The same was applicable to Pepsi Cola 50cl bottles from 35cl before Coca-Cola copied it and even went further to introduce 60cls bottles.

Credible and incisive market research will be useful or required in providing answers to most of these questions. Creativity, ingenuity, and originality in responding to customers on some of these issues will be the real demarcating factor for the brand. This is so because the issues raised may be the same for all the brands operating in the same market sector, but how each brand chooses to creatively approach them will be as unique as the brand, and it is this uniqueness of approach that may end up endearing the brand to their customers.

A brand that seeks to succeed in the marketplace does not have any choice but to be extremely responsive to its customers. Else it is doomed to fail. This is more so as it is the person that pays the piper that dictates the tune. A good example that one can readily draw from baring many years of exposure to the brand is Coca-Cola. Based on its distribution and sales process, you have a minimum of four different levels of employees whose only work on a daily basis is to visit the market and provide the best brand response to different market issues on a regular basis.

You have the merchandisers whose only job is to visit specific outlets and ensure that the various Coca-Cola products are not only well but also visibly well displayed in the various outlets in line with the brand standards. They also ensure that the brand gets prominence in the various shelf displays and can actually help the outlet owner carry out such displays.

Secondly is the salesperson, whose job it is to supply the outlets and ensure that there is no stock out but that the buffer stock required to take care of any spike in demand is available. Above them are the supervisors whose job is to ensure within a geographical area that all these things are complied with and finally the sales manager. Each of these personnel embarks on routine outlet visits and, as part of their job, does ensure that the chillers and other assets of the organization in the outlet are 100 percent deployed for the company's products. Any infringement of these standards by the outlet can lead to various sanctions and possible withdrawal of the company's assets.

Brand Relevance

Relevance refers to how appropriate something is to what is being done or said at a given time. Brand relevance, therefore, refers to how appropriate your brand is to your customer's or consumer's life and lifestyle. Brand relevance is a relatively new concept in brand management. What used to be the more prevalent concept was brand preference.

Brand preference reflects a desire to opt for, choose or select and use a particular company's products or services, even when there are equally priced and equally available alternatives. Sometimes it refers to a desire to seek out a specific product or service, even when it requires paying more or expending more effort to obtain it. It is a good indicator of the customers' loyalty, the strength of the brand, and an indicator of the level of success of the company's marketing efforts and tactics over the years.

Brand relevance, however, is a much deeper concept because except the brand can maintain its relevance as new categories and subcategories emerge, change or fade, no amount of marketing or brand investment will sustain its preference in the market. According to Clayton M. Christensen, brand managers may be blindsided by changing product categories primarily because they focus too closely on the traditional attributes of brands within their old categories such that they may achieve preference and differentiation for their brands only to have that effort wasted as the entire product category within which they have invested their whole efforts in fades overnight thereby creating a huge relevance problem for them.

Brand relevance has become key, bearing in mind the phenomenally dynamic changes taking place in the market currently where no product or service category is spared or immune from such changes. Consumers and even corporate buyers are better informed about every possible trend or occurrence in the market than ever before. They are mobile and are increasingly able to get precisely what they want when they want it, and at a price they're willing to pay for it. As a result of this trend, new categories and subcategories appear and disappear almost overnight. In such situations where old categories are undermined, augmented, replaced, or subsumed by a new, faster-growing category, no amount of brand investment in such a dwindling category will be able to sustain the loyalty, trust, and esteem of the customers. In such a situation, something needs to be done to the brand to sustain its relevance to the market.

According to David Aaker, companies have three options: to either be trend neglecters, trend drivers, or trend responders. Neglecting trends is a risky road that often leads to oblivion; trend driving, with its huge upside, is certainly attractive but rarely a real option. Most firms need to learn to be good trend responders and build the organizational skills to detect, evaluate, and react to change, and develop a well-conceived brand portfolio strategy.

Relevance for a brand, therefore, occurs when three conditions are met:

- A product or service category or subcategory—defined by some combination of attributes, applications, user groups, or other distinguishing characteristics—exists or emerges.

- There is a perceived need or desire on the part of a customer segment for the category or subcategory.

- The brand is in the set that the segment considers material for the product category or subcategory.

David Aaker, in his phenomenal work on brand relevance, distinguished between categories associated with a brand and brands associated with a category. According to him, what is more important is to know brands that are associated with a specific product category or subcategory as opposed to knowing categories that are associated with the brand. For instance, when you mention Lexus 570 cars which product category or subcategory comes to mind. It is not as important to know that Lexus cars are associated with luxury as it is to know that Lexus 570 typifies the optimum luxury class.

Recalling a brand, therefore, as an epitome of a product category without any aid is the apt definition or classification of relevance. Subsequently also, visibility alone, no matter how prominent, is not sufficient to maintain the relevance of the brand since the roof might already have been taken off from the product category that the brand represents.

According to Prophet, the ad agency, brands with relevance inspire us and move us to action. Everything the brand invests in, creates, or brings to the market is designed to meet important needs in peoples' lives. They also make sure that their products are available where and when customers need them, deliver consistent experiences and simply make life easier for their customers. They also make emotional connections, earn trust, and often exist to fulfill a larger purpose. Even as industry leaders, these brands don't rest on their laurels. They still push the status quo, engage with customers in new and creative ways, find ways to address unmet needs, and often redefine the market and even the competition.

Apt examples of brand relevance are two local transport companies that have been able to distinguish themselves among several other transport companies in their particular product categories. The two transport companies are Autostar and Peace Mass Transit.

Peace Mass Transit started up in a sector that was both competitive and littered with so many individual small-scale operators. The cutting edge for them to both maintain relevance and redefine the category—mass transit was speed, scale, and price. Due to the small scale and individualized nature of local mass transit companies, they usually did not have enough fleet of cars to carry all the teeming population in need of movement such that a lot of passenger waiting time was being experienced. The proprietor focused on developing a huge fleet base to cater to this population. He also developed unique routes that people were not usually plying, which not only created avenues of deployment for his buses but also made a huge profit for him. He finally brought down the prices of transport fares such that passengers can now afford to travel to their destinations without being overloaded.

Autostar, on the other hand, adopted a completely different and unique strategy, which also made them create and dominate their niche. The proprietor identified the need for luxury travel on the road for select passengers who will want a comfortable alternative to the airlines. For such passengers, he developed the concept of using Toyota Sienna buses as opposed to the usual Coaster or hummer buses. The Sienna as a family car is roomier, cozier, and more comfortable. The suspensions and shock absorbers of the cars were more ideal for our bad roads as they could withstand bumps better than the regular buses. He restricted the number of passengers per bus to five, which was classy such that you had more than enough legroom and space for relaxation without bumping into the next passenger as opposed to the regular buses.

The apparent success of the Autostar concept saw the deluge of other transporters mimicking or adopting the same strategy such that several other transporters started using the same Sienna buses for such executive services. However, in seeking to sustain the relevance of his brand, he focused on his drivers, who he spent time to train and acculturate to represent the brand ethos of the organization. There was very strict adherence to the speed limit of 100 kilometers per hour such that regardless of the pressure or road rage, the drivers were found to conform strictly to the speed limit. This gave a huge assurance of safety to the customers with reduced worry or concern about accidents. The organization, in also seeking to remain relevant to their customers, upscaled their operation by adopting a customized INNOSON bus as a distinguishing factor from all the other companies who copied their Sienna buses concept.

At the end of the day, relevance refers to being the most appropriate brand for your customers and consumers within a particular product category or subcategory or having your brand being recognized as the most appropriate brand for that category.

Recalling a brand therefore, as an epitome of a product category without any aid is the apt definition or classification of relevance.

Subsequently also visibility alone no matter how prominent is not sufficient to maintain the relevance of the brand since the roof might already have been taken off from the product category that the brand represents.

Brand Governance
The principal role of brand governance is to ensure that brands are presented consistently, that guidelines are properly followed and executed, and that rules are followed. It refers to the manner in which power is exercised in the management of a brand or the rules of the brand system to solve conflicts between actors or major proponents of the brand.

Governance is also the process of decision-making and the process by which decisions are implemented (or not implemented). An analysis of governance focuses on the formal and informal actors involved in decision-making and implementing the decisions made and the formal and informal structures that have been set in place to arrive at and implement the decision.

In other words, what are the rules and control measures that the brand owners set for the brand such that the brand can grow unhindered and achieve its objectives and full potential as a brand? This is akin to charting a course, direction, and path for the brand, which, if adopted, will surely lead it to the point of achievement of its objectives or dreams as a brand.

As brands grow and extend themselves, there has to exist some form of governance or control principle that determines what falls within the purview of the brand or outside of it. Otherwise, the brand will lose its essence, meaning as well as direction. Finding a glue or common proposition that holds all the brand variants together as well as ensuring that each of them delivers a consistent promised quality of brand experience across so many brand variants is a task that clearly requires a strong governance principle.

Brands also, in their channel selections and forging of strategic alliances such as franchising, subcontracting, licensing, or joint ownership, have to come up with very clear governance principles and guidelines so as not to dilute or lose the meaning and essence of their brand completely. These principles ensure that the partnerships are with like-minded people who also have the same level of commitment to the brand ideals. Nothing could be worse than going to bed with strange bedfellows who have opposite thoughts, views, and perceptions of important principles and may not agree on the best way to move forward.

Most brands have a clearly set out standard for their brand (brand manuals), ranging from how it is written or deployed in different platforms; letter headed papers, T-shirts, etc.; the color combinations for the brand down to the correct Pantone chart colors; what the brand can be associated or not associated with and for consumer goods product, the allowable display patterns or style on trade, etc.

From experience, these standards—as good and as very nice as they are or might be—conformance or adherence to them might be the key factor and not just the mere fact that there are rules in existence. Ensuring compliance among the key brand actors ranging from the printers (below the line vendors etc.) who cut corners, seek for short cuts, and deviations from the standards so as to maximize or increase their profit margins and the various salesmen and women who, although knowledgeable about these standards, may not want to embark on the extra hard work required to achieve them, hence the bid to cut corners is the major challenge of brand governance.

In view of all these, how do the brand owners and managers ensure that the brand is not diluted and the brand standards complied with? Some organizations have organized different layers of supervision and certification of these standards so as to ensure compliance. These layers often range from the supervisors, sales managers, and regional managers to marketing managers and, at the apex, the brand council that has an overall say in whatever concerns the brand.

Ideas can emanate from whichever level within the organization if the organization itself is well structured, but such ideas with regards to the brand cannot be implemented without the formal sign-off of the brand council. That way, the brand enjoys some level of stability and does not suffer from the hiccups of individual, irrational or emotional responses to the brand based on personal proclivities and tendencies.

One of the major advantages or benefits of brand governance has been to ensure that the brand is seen the way it wants to be seen and to ensure consistency in its messaging, look, and feel. This is important because of the particular impression the brand wants to make in the minds of its customers, which is dependent on the way the brand is viewed or perceived by its customers and consumers. A brand, by merely looking at it or the way it is presented, might convey the perception of a committed, diligent and painstaking brand or an unserious brand.

The current digital age has posed a huge challenge to exactly how far the brand owners can control the brand. As a matter of fact, the issue of who actually owns the brand, the customers, or the brand manufacturers has also become an increasing point of discussion. This is so because the digital age has given the consumers and customers a very easy way of having access as well as valid input into designing and influencing both the nature as well as the message of the brand. Examples of famous brand parodies and other forms of messaging, both good and bad, have dotted the brand landscape with huge impacts also. According to Christina de Balanzo, "brands actually belong to people, not marketing," as they live in the minds of those who regularly interact with them.

For Eirik Ekrann, brand governance is the bridge between brand strategy formulation in the boardroom and the actual execution in the field. Operationalizing the brand strategy not only provides a credible basis for evaluating the brand between what it set out to achieve and what it eventually achieved but also acts as a check as to whether the brand strategy is too ambiguous, complex, or fluffy.

According to the UN definition, there are eight major characteristics of good governance. It must be participatory, consensus-oriented, accountable, transparent, responsive, effective and efficient, equitable and inclusive, and follows the rule of law. If governance rules are dictated, they will be dictatorial and will lack the necessary ingredient to mobilize or galvanize everyone around the same goals and objectives. At the same time, it cannot be a *laissez-faire* scenario where every possible view or perspective is allowed, or else a monumental confusion will ensue.

Landor, in their landmark study, developed the Brand Community Model as a means of governing the brand. The brand community model was predicated on two main premises; that all the brand audiences cannot be treated the same way, as they all do not have the same level of knowledge and expertise with regards to the brand. The second premise is that all brand expressions cannot be treated the same way, as they all do not have the same level of importance.

They identified three levels of people that play a vital role in shaping the brand; the experts, the practitioners, and the employees. They also identified three levels of brand expressions; the sacred, the interpretative, and the exploratory. The experts refer to the organizational leadership, brand, and marketing teams as well as the agency partners. They are the real custodians of the brand, understand the reason behind all that the brand does and define the future of the brand as well as its strategy. Very important and overriding decisions about the brand should be handled at this level.

The practitioners are the group of people who have the primary responsibilities of implementing the brand decisions in the marketplace, like the various cadres of salespeople, supervisors, managers, client service personnel, etc. They understand some of the reasons behind what the brand does but do not have very intricate knowledge about the brand. As people charged with the responsibility of brand implementation, they can come up with very valid feedback that can be incorporated into the very salient decisions about the brand, which will be highly beneficial to the brand.

The third level of people in the brand community other than the consumers are the employees of the brand organization. These people, although they are not concerned with the brand conceptualization or implementation on a day-to-day basis, are still ambassadors of the brand as they interface in the frontline with the various users of the brand. They wear the cloak of the brand as employees and, as such, must exhibit the full brand ethos and essence, speak on behalf of the brand, advocate for it and also respond appropriately to customer requests, etc. This, therefore, calls for concerted efforts of brand education and indoctrination for the employees.

Interfacing with these three levels of the brand community are the three levels of brand expressions. The sacred levels of brand expressions refer to the various verbal, visual, behavioral, experiential elements of the brand that fundamentally defines it. These are the core or the real essence of the brand without which the brand ceases to be what it is and becomes a different entity altogether. They are therefore inviolable and cannot be compromised. Decisions about this level of brand elements are the exclusive preserve of the experts in the brand community—the leadership, brand and marketing team, etc.

The interpretative level of the brand expressions includes those elements that can be adapted based on context, market, or geography without deviating from the brand essence. This is mainly to give room for growth, responsiveness, and dynamism or agility in the brand. Different communities express interest and ownership of the brand in different ways. In acknowledging such levels of endearment from the communities, certain peculiar aspects of the culture of these localities can be integrated into the brand as a means of expressing the same-shared values between the brand and such communities. This creates an affinity between the two— the brand and the community that will be in the mutual interest of both.

The exploratory aspects of the brand are those aspects of the brand that can be opened up to creativity and risk. An example has been different brands asking their various customers to phone in, record, or photograph their famous moments/ interactions with the brand so as to win a prize, etc. This normally leads to the various individuals' expressions of their own values or attachments to the brand, which may both be unexpected and previously unimagined by the brand team and, as such, may not have been incorporated into the brand wheel of expressions or value. Some of these explorations may also turn out to be very inspiring and breakthrough moments for the brand. The benefit in adopting such an approach is that the brand is not directly involved in any of those expressions, and any inimical expression can always be shut down, discouraged, or distanced from the brand as opposed to a scenario where the brand itself is involved in such expressions.

This approach of brand governance creates a loop where all the various essential players are actively involved in the management or governance of the brand based on their level of expertise and impact. The ones with the major expertise and knowledge operate from the core, whereas those with lower levels of knowledge and expertise about the brand operate from the periphery.

This approach also dimensions the level of impact that such involvements can have on the brand. The maximum impact comes from the center, and even if any danger comes from the various levels of participation and expressions from the other levels within the community, it can always be isolated, and the negative impact on the brand is reduced to the barest minimum.

Each group of the brand community can be called upon or charged with responsibilities that are more akin to their expertise. If a brand does not develop or adopt very clear governance principles in its management, the brand might not live long or survive the deluge of confusion that might bedevil it, thereby leading to an early demise. Another major reason why brands fail is due to a **LACK OF STRATEGIC FOCUS OR APPROACH** in the management of the brand. Brands like every other marketing arsenal can be deployed or built up strategically or tactically with a long-term or short-term focus, or they can be built up haphazardly.

If you jump into branding without much thought or consideration about what you want to achieve and how you want to achieve them, you will most likely end up with a brand that is misaligned or a vague, unimpactful, forgettable, or worse still, a confused brand. However, when you go through a thoughtful branding process, your company or organization can emerge with a powerful articulation of why your work matters, as well as a vehicle that will mobilize others to get on board.

To be able to manage strategically, it needs to be understood that brands are strategic assets that can be deployed to achieve a particular business objective and also that brands have value or equity.

A brand like Apple is worth about $260.2 billion according to 2020 Forbes brand valuation, while Google is worth about $145.6 billion. It is only a brand like Apple that can charge $999 for a phone and end up selling about 29 million pieces of the phone. Coca-Cola brand, on the other hand, is worth about $57.3 billion according to the 2018 Forbes brand valuation. This can only be put in perspective when we compare these brand valuations with the revised 2020 Nigerian budget of N10.51 trillion or $29.19 billion. A brand like Apple is worth approximately nine times the Nigerian annual budget. You definitely will not want to play or take such brands for granted. With a market valuation of $1.95 trillion, it is bigger than the GDP of Canada, Russia, or Spain.

When you realize that brands have huge value and can amount to huge monetary value, your perspective or approach to managing such a brand will automatically change. Brands are also strategic assets in that the deployment or variations in the deployment of such brands can tilt the equation or equilibrium for any organization to the positive or negative. There are fighter and defender brands with different roles and functions in the market such that the introduction or withdrawal of the brands in the market can alter the market dynamics at different points in time. If brand owners do not know the strengths and value of their brands as well as their capabilities in the market, the full benefits of those brands will not be realized.

In deciding on what will be the most suitable or ideal strategy for the brand, which will automatically lead to the amount of effort and eventual pay off from the brand, the brand owner will have to answer a series of questions. According to Duanne Kapp, some of which are; what is distinctive about our products or services, who are your customers and whose perceptions are key to the brand in achieving its objectives, what are the key things you will want your customers to think about you or the perceptions you want them to have about you? How do you get your message across to them about who you are and get them to believe and trust your brand?

At the end of the day, some hard-nosed internal assessments, competitive analysis, and marketing and market research will be required as key inputs into your brand-building activities. Three key parties that are usually involved or critical in the brand-building effort are the internal stakeholders (staff, employees, management, etc.), the external stakeholders (customers, consumers, regulatory agencies, media agencies, investors, etc.), and the group of people who are charged with the responsibilities of obtaining, analyzing and interpreting information about the brand as well as utilizing this information in arriving at brand-building initiatives.

As a matter of fact, a key tool of brand building is comprehensive stakeholder analysis and how each of these key stakeholders perceives and responds or reacts to the brand. In other words, the brand interfaces differently with different stakeholders and harnessing all these reactions into a melting point that will determine the brand's approach to these key stakeholders in general and specifically is critical in a strategic approach of building the brand. (the bus driver and the banker will definitely not interface with your brand in exactly the same way)

This comprehensive stakeholder analysis usually dovetails into a touchpoint analysis. According to Stein & Ramaseshan, touchpoints can be defined as any of the various ways that a consumer can or does interact with your brand, whether it be person-to-person, through a website, an app, or any form of communication. When consumers come in contact with these touchpoints, it gives them the opportunity to compare their prior perceptions of the brand and form an opinion.

According to Pantano and Viassone, touchpoints are critical because they allow customers to have experiences every time they "touch" any part of the product, service, brand, or organization across multiple channels and various points in time. These contacts with the customers at the various touchpoints shape and influence the customer's opinions and perceptions either positively or negatively, depending wholly on the individuals.

Touchpoints also have the ability to influence consumers' buying or intent to purchase, all throughout the five stages of the buyer purchasing decision-making process. Touchpoints can therefore be designed in such a way that it is a message or a means whereby the brand reaches out to their target market, providing engagement as it allows the brand to be seen by the prospective customer in a favorable way.

The whole essence of this touchpoint analysis or design is such that it creates an opportunity for the purchaser to choose a particular brand over another competitor. If a brand provides better excitement and engagement than other brands on its website, for instance, customers and consumers will more likely pay more visits to the brand's website than that of their competitors.

This is the thinking behind the approach of most fashion designers where they encourage their customers to provide their own unique customization or designs for their desired products, and that customization will be produced for them. This not only creates excitement but also encourages the customer's patronage and engagement based on the feeling that the organization is responsive to their needs and allows them to express themselves uniquely. Over time this creates a huge horde of brand loyalists and ambassadors, whereas the brands will benefit from these unique creative ideas in their future creations.

Touchpoints are also a powerful tool of reaching out to the customers as it allows the brands owners the use of specific communication tools and designs to reach the appropriate target audience, thereby making room for their uniqueness and differences as opposed to using one general tool for all their audience without any variations.

Touchpoints are also useful in that they provide prospective customers with specific or more useful information on their brands which allows them to become more knowledgeable on the brand and the benefits offered while allowing them to make a decision on whether they will buy the product or service.

With such a deliberate and strategic approach to managing the brand, brand building will no longer be a haphazard activity or approach where whatever whimsical thought or feelings that crosses the CEO or the brand manager's mind will be converted to a series of different brand-related activities. Any such whimsical and not deliberate or strategic approach to brand building is a sure recipe for failure. Brands are strategic assets with huge values that need to be carefully and deliberately nurtured to achieve the brand goals.

CHAPTER SIX

Differentiation, Distinctiveness and Salience

There would not have been any need for differentiation if all the products and brands were the same or were intended to be the same. The world would have been a monotonous place if there were no differences. Human choice is based on the premise of differences between two or more objects hence the need for man to select or choose from all the available options. To be able to make such choices, the consumers must be provided with valid reasons or premises that will warrant such a decision or choice between a particular product or services and the other alternative goods and services.

If this is so, why then do we have commodity markets and products, which are largely undifferentiated like oil, mining, and agricultural products making so much money and profits from their operations? For these money-making corporations who are into commodity products, it is the operations, structures, and systems put in place by the corporate brand and the efficiency they bring into their operations that enables the firms to make money. For example, why do you prefer to buy or refuel your car at specific petrol filling stations despite the fact that the products being sold by all the petrol filling stations are the same and at the same price?

Why also are not all the petrol filling stations equally profitable? At the end of the day, it is still the differences engineered into the operations of those organizations that translate into making a commodity product more distinguishable, preferable, and more profitable than another.

Beyond that, for all commodities, there are standards of evaluation or pre-inspection standards to ensure that they conform to certain basic standards. These standards have grading systems attached to them such that some are prime A-class products just the same way some crude oil is preferred in the market and subsequently attracts higher prices. At the end of the day, despite the fact that there are similarities between the commodities, there still exists classifications and differences among them; a selection process where the best products attract a different price from the remaining ones. These A-class products usually end up being sold first before the rest products. Consequently, some level of differentiation still exists in commodities either as a result of the quality or geographical location that they are produced from or their species etc.

One of the very valid arguments for differentiation is that it leads to higher profits. Sharp and Dawes defined differentiation as when a firm/brand outperforms rival brands in the provision of a feature(s) such that it faces reduced sensitivity for other feature(s). For not having to provide these other features, the firm, therefore, has an avenue to save costs. This reduced sensitivity also allows the firm/brand to benefit from a reduced intensity or directness of competition, thereby enabling it access to portions of the market or the value created by the exchange.

Kotler, on his own part, defined differentiation as "the act of designing a set of meaningful differences to distinguish the company's offer from competitors' offers."

Differentiation can therefore exist at different levels, at the corporate strategic level or at the operational and tactical levels. It can also exist at the product/brand level, at the engineering or process level of the firm, at the level of the distribution and the other elements of the marketing p's, or at the level of the personnel and employees of the firm; customer service/ after-sales service.

Levels of Differentiation
Differentiation does not only exist at the level of the product or brand. Differentiation can exist at the level of the company (Corporate, Strategic) level where the company's or institutional positioning forms a very clear form of differentiation between all the products and brands emanating from the different organizations.

Patagonia, as a niche sports equipment and wares manufacturer, was able to differentiate itself from all other sports equipment manufacturers based on various environmental sustainability efforts as well as their wares that were made to last.

Other manufacturers like Vita Coconut oils which do not use monkeys in their coconut farming, became 100 percent vegan and cruelty-free and were able to differentiate themselves based on their policy of not patronizing or using coconuts harvested using forced or chained monkeys. Some diamond manufacturers have also differentiated themselves by not buying and selling "blood diamonds." Based on these differentiations, any product or brand that emanates from their staid will be looked upon differently with a different inclination by the buyers, which oftentimes disposes them toward purchasing their products.

Differentiation can also be at the operational level encompassing all aspects of the production; distribution, selling, and customer service touchpoints. At each of these points lays infinite possibilities in differentiating one organization from another. Nigerian Breweries bottlers of Heineken in Nigeria at one point in time took a huge leap in installing the largest production line in Africa in one of their production sites known as AMA Breweries. This was at a point when they were upscaling their facilities against the incursion of SAB Miller from South Africa. The magnitude of the production line, as well as the scale of efficiency, was a very clear differentiating factor in their operations. FedEx, when they also were trying to differentiate themselves in the market, embarked on a very innovative scheme, which had not been operational in the market—Overnight deliveries. This distribution mechanism was a huge factor in differentiating the organization, even if it was later copied by other organizations.

Differentiation can also exist at the tactical level bearing in mind the differences either in the culture and way of life of the consumers, which the organization can incorporate into their operations in specific locations so as to create a differentiation between their product offerings and that of their competitors.

The biggest mistake, therefore in differentiation, is to think that it must exist at the level of the product features and characteristics, which must be engineered into the product to differentiate it from other products within its target market. Product differentiation is good. However, if they don't or if they are very easily copied by competitors as they will normally be, then other avenues for differentiation that the company can explore in seeking to differentiate their product offerings abound if only they will look deeply enough. One veritable means of arriving at these areas of differences are through research.

What then is Differentiation?
One very good explanation of differentiation is that by Dawn

Laccobucci, which says that Brand differentiation operates mainly by facilitating buyer learning. Buyers are constantly in search of product offerings to meet their needs as well as reasons or basis for selecting or choosing one product above another. Differentiation is thereby a means whereby the owners of the brand seeks to educate, inform or make the buyer aware of the inherent differences and benefits among their product offerings that are either not present among their competitors' offerings or that distinguishes them from them, thereby forming a credible basis of being chosen above their competitors.

Different theories of buyer behavior exist, ranging from the ones that believe that the buyer is not aware of what he or she wants and as such that it is the responsibility of the marketing communication process to make them aware of such needs, to the ones that believe that the buyer is highly rational and focused with a very clear understanding of what he or she wants such that the role of the marketing communication process is to make aware to the customer what they are offering as a means of easing the search and elimination process for the buyer based on the specifications he already has and wants to fill.

Whichever school of buyer behavior one is inclined to, the basic fact still remains that there are certain criteria, characteristics, or differences that the buyer is looking for; the presence or absence of it will determine whether the buyer will or will not buy a specific product offering. If the owners of the brands understand their buyers' needs effectively, then the entire production, distribution, and marketing process will therefore be attuned toward meeting these needs of the buyer by highlighting those differences that are appealing to him or her on which basis the buyer purchase decision will be based upon. Differentiation, according to Hinge University, is simply not about showcasing ephemeral differences or about being different for the sake of being different. It's about helping your audience make smarter, easier, more confident buying decisions. Differentiation is also about what your product or service does /accomplishes/ offers that the competition does not? Or what makes them more appealing to customers than other options in your category?

Some of the basic elements that you can use in differentiating your products and services are quality, design, service and interactions/ touchpoints, features and functionalities of the products, customization, etc.

Product and Brand Differentiation
In talking about differentiation, we will look at it from two different perspectives: product differentiation and brand differentiation. Product differentiation refers to the engineering aspect of the product where you engineer specific attributes and differences into your product, whereas brand differentiation is the means by which your brand is set apart from the competition by associating a superior performing aspect of your brand with multiple customer benefits. A system whereby everything within the brand's wheel or circumference around the product other than just the features— which have a capacity of making indelible impressions in the minds of the consumers—are used as a basis of differentiation.

In product differentiation, you build specific attributes into the product, whereas in brand differentiation, you associate these product attributes and characteristics to the customers' benefits and aspirations or need such that this association or positioning, as we will see later, makes the brand the preferable option for the customers.

The difference between product and brand differentiation speaks to the major differences between the two; a product and a brand.

According to Kapferer, you buy a product for what it does while you choose a brand for what it means. A product sits on the retailers' shelves, whereas a brand exists in the consumers' minds. A product can be quickly outdated, whereas a brand is timeless. A product can be copied by a competitor, whereas a brand is unique and defies copying.

A product, therefore, becomes or attains the status of a brand when the physical product is augmented by something else—images, symbols, perceptions, feelings, etc.—to produce an integral idea greater than the sum of its parts. This augmentation process, as opposed to the actual engineering and production of the product, is the major difference between product differentiation and brand differentiation.

Three Key Factors in Differentiation

Product differentiation encompasses three different things; the creation of a difference that has the capability of differentiating the company's products and services from that of their competitors; identifying and communicating these differences or unique qualities and attributes and the development of a strong value proposition that will be attractive or captivating to the customers

For every product or service, there is a very wide area or space within which the product or service can wish to differentiate itself. These areas borders on two main dimensions, the five levels of the product ranging from the core benefit, the generic product, the expected product, the augmented product and the potential product, and the different target customers (their characteristics, needs and wants). When you interplay these two factors, it gives you an infinite possibility within which one can differentiate the products and services. There are different customer groups, and each of these customer groups is so diverse in what they want and also on the various product and service options that can appeal to them or meet their needs so long as their number is sizeable enough to warrant profits for the business. Critical therefore is the knowledge of the customers, your willingness, and your ability to meet their needs. Once the necessary knowledge, competence, and resources to meet the customer's needs exist, then there will be numerous options of engineering or incorporating differences into the products or services so as to differentiate them.

The beauty and personal care segment of the market is one huge example. The soap market, a sub-segment of the market, is also a good case in point. Numerous uncountable brands of soaps exist in the market, each with its different differentiation. Under it, you have different bathing bars with attractive colors and fragrances, claiming to have moisturizing, skin whitening, and anti-aging effects under different brand names and differentiations with their key target customers.

The second aspect of differentiation involves identifying and communicating these differences or unique qualities and attributes of the product or service, especially due to the fact that these differences might be opaque and not immediately visible to the customers such that if you do not highlight or buttress them, they might not know about it nor even be attracted to it.

According to Josh Porter, the key to communicating your products or services value is to identify how they resonate or apply to the individual personally and emotionally, as well as the benefits it offers them. The customer is usually and mostly interested in finding out; what is in it for me and how does that make me feel or look better or improve my life? As long as you can establish this deep connection, emphasize them in a creative, clear, and emphatic manner, consistently over a period of time, the chances are that you will gain a little ground in the customer's mind, which is all you need to get a foot in the door.

The third aspect of differentiation involves developing a strong value proposition that will be attractive or captivating to the customers. A value proposition, according to Casey Newman, is a statement that answers the 'why' someone should do business with you. It should convince a potential customer why your service or product will be of more value to them than similar offerings from your competition. It also makes the benefits of your products or services very clear from the onset. In a nutshell, a value proposition refers to the value that a company promises to deliver to customers should they choose to buy their products.

As a business, you might know or have all the reasons why your products and services are of better quality than that of your competitors (if you didn't think they were better, chances are you may not have ventured into the business); however, your potential customers are not aware of any of all these facts. It is the basis on which your customers evaluate your products and services, and usually one of the first things that they seek to know or find out—how are you different or what different values do you offer different from your competitors? Consequently, making these reasons available to them eases the hassles for them. It also facilitates the choice as well as the decision-making process.

The simple and most outstanding way of evaluating your value proposition is how it lines up or solves the customers' most important problem or need for wanting those products or services. To be able to do that, you need to understand the customers' pain point, the benefits that your products and services offer and how it best meets those customers' needs. Failure to do that will only lead to an empty rambling that will do no good or bring any benefits.

As a matter of fact, your value proposition should be the nexus or the confluence point between your products/ services benefits and the needs of the customers; the product/service that best understands and meets their needs in the most creative and efficient manner wins the day.

A good example of one such good value proposition is Uber—"The smartest way to get around." For such value propositions to be effective, they have to be very clear, simple, and straightforward, almost with a single-minded appeal so as to avoid confusion or being crowded with too much information.

It also needs to be provable or backed up with proofs or experiences that users of such products and services can confirm or identify with. No wonder Uber is so bent on their driver's evaluation and always follows up to confirm your satisfaction after a trip, and if there is a stoppage along the way, they will immediately get in touch with you to find out the cause of such delays.

The Concept of Perceived Value in the Customer Decision-Making Process

When a customer evaluates a product with a view to purchasing it, they always weigh the perceived value of the product versus the price of the product.

> *A value proposition refers to the value that a company promises to deliver to customers should they choose to buy their products.*

The product's perceived value is, therefore, one of the most important consideration factors by the customers in evaluating the product. The problem, however, is that the true value of a product is very difficult to understand or determine due to its psychological and extremely personal nature. At the end of the day, the actual amount of value inherent in a product is dependent on the individual, although there are functional and emotional elements that are associated with a product's value that can assist the customer in determining its true value.

Despite this difficulty in determining the true value of a product, it can still be the major building block to a successful marketing campaign if correctly done, so it is very crucial to understand which elements shape your product's core value so as to improve it and use it as a basis of making you stand out from the competition.

According to Almquist, Senior, and Bloch (2016), there are thirty building blocks or elements of value that determine the product's value and consequently influence the customer's decision-making process. These building blocks are represented in a pyramid form and fall into four different categories: functional, emotional, life-changing, and social impact. At the bottom are the values associated with the most common physical needs, while the higher up the pyramid you have, the more complex and harder to implement elements climaxing with the self-transcendence level. The value pyramid agrees largely with the principles behind Maslow's hierarchy of needs.

At the functional level of the value, which is at the bottom of the pyramid, you have attributes like; saving time, simplifying, making money, reducing risk, organizing, integrating, connecting, reducing effort, avoiding hassles, reducing cost, quality, variety, sensory appeal and informs. At the emotional level, you have attributes like wellness, therapeutic value, fun/entertainment, attractiveness, provides access, reduces anxiety, rewards me, nostalgia, design/aesthetics, and badge value. Life-changing values, which are at the third level, involve the provision of hope, self-actualization, motivation, heirloom, and affiliation/belonging, while at the apex of the pyramid, you have self-transcendence.

When you consider a product attribute as important, you have to clearly specify why you consider it to be important. So when talking about convenience, for instance, the person might be referring to a set of underlining values like time-saving, avoiding hassles, simplifying the process and reducing effort. At the same time, the usage of a Lamborghini might underline some life-changing elements like self-actualization in using a car for such an amount of money that exudes self-expression and actualization.

Some elements of the values are more inwardly focused, primarily addressing consumers' personal needs, while others are outwardly focused, aimed at helping customers interact with or navigate the external world. The functional elements of perceived value, for instance, help consumers deal with complexities in their world. So when you consider or rate a product attribute as important, you have to be sure what aspect and how many of the elements of value it speaks to.

According to the study, the higher the elements you choose and deliver, the faster you'll be able to grow and have profit. Strategic organizations understand how they stack up against competitors on these value elements and have methodically chosen new elements of this value to incorporate into their products over time as a means of differentiating themselves from their competitors. The more of these values they introduce into their product offerings or services, the more game changers they become and the more they widen the gap or create more points of differentiation between them and their competitors.

However, to be able to differentiate yourself (product or services) on these higher-order elements, you first need to have a strong foundation and provide at least some of the functional elements, one of which is quality. Products and services must attain a certain minimum level of perceived quality before they can ever seek to position themselves on whatever other higher pedestal. No other elements can make up for a significant shortfall in quality. If these basic values are not met, you won't be able to make an emotional and psychological connection with your customer (Amado, 2019).

The study by Almquist, Senior, and Bloch also showed that the companies that performed well on multiple elements of value would have more loyal customers than the rest. Although it is impossible to inject the thirty elements of value into a single product or service, companies must therefore choose the elements of value to incorporate into their products and service strategically based on what are the most valuable attributes in their market segment.

Part of the challenge of the product strategy, therefore, is to identify and come up with the right combination of value building blocks that are considered the most important within your industry such that your product can deliver the best value to your customers. The endpoint of all these differentiation activities is to confer a competitive advantage to the products or services. To be able to arrive at this competitive advantage or for the identified product attributes to confer a competitive advantage to the product, the target audience must also be taken into consideration.

For instance, what are those qualities or attributes which customers or consumers within that target market consider as critical or very important? What are those attributes that are important to them that they will consider a winning edge for whatever product or service that has them? What are their views and conceptions of a good product? What are the basic needs and wants of these target segments that they will want to meet through the usage of these products and services? What is the total population as well as the purchasing power of these target segments or the proportion that considers such needs critical? This is important because if the number of those who want or are crazy about those qualities and attributes are not many, then it would have amounted to a wild goose chase since the effort put into trying to build such attributes into the products or services will not return the desired income from the investment that actualized it. If the numbers of the target customers are not much, but they have a significant purchasing power, then the product or services can qualify as a specialty product targeted at a select few with the purchasing power to acquire them.

It is also important to note that what is or confers a competitive advantage to a product today may cease to offer the same competitive advantage as the customers may no longer consider those attributes as critical. One popular example is the Polaroid and Kodak cameras that could snap and print pictures immediately. As fanciful and as colorful as that was for that time, it ceased to have a competitive advantage once digital cameras came into being. All the rolls of films that were required to take pictures, whether they were faster, more colorful, easier to handle, cheaper, etc., all vanished with the twinkling of an eye rendered obsolete by digital cameras.

Today's competitive advantage may cease to offer the same competitive advantage tomorrow owing to two facts; changes or shifts in the customers' taste or the development of new and innovative products as a result of some new and disruptive technology. For products or services to enjoy any competitive advantage upon which it will hope to differentiate itself, there must be a constant effort at updating the product, the technology behind it, or even the development of new products and services from research and development. The car industry has remained dynamic because every year, new designs based on improved performance, ergonomics, and technology advancements will inundate the market across all segments such that it could even be a rat race for the customers to keep up.

Differentiators and their test
In trying to determine or settle on these differentiators or value building blocks that will be used as a basis for differentiating the product or services, they must pass through certain screening or tests to confirm their validity.

According to John Tyreman, the first criterion in evaluating differentiators is whether those differentiators or claims about them are true! The easiest way to lose credibility as a product is for your customers on usage or contact with your product to realize that the product's claims or assertions are not true or as significant as presented. This will discourage repeat purchases as well as elicit a flood of negative word-of-mouth advertising, which will be the surest way of killing not only the reputation of the product or service but the product itself.

This point of evaluation will also be a good point to eliminate or discard product claims that are generic and not peculiar or unique to your product or services. Uniqueness and veracity is, therefore, the first test that any attribute, quality, or assertion that you want to claim about your product or services must have. If not, the differentiators will already be standing on shaky grounds and will not muster enough energy or force to influence or convince the customers to patronize your products.

The second criterion for evaluating the differentiators and how well they can make an impact in the market is how ascertainable or provable those claims are? Are they visible to the eyes, or must you use them to be able to ascertain them, or are they just credence values that you want the customers to believe do exist, as they are not too easy to prove? For instance, are those advantages embedded in the production process of the products and services such that they are not visible or capable of being immediately experienced? If the impact of those product benefits is not easily ascertained, it will be difficult to convince the customer to believe in a phantom. Over time, doubts and disbelief will creep in, and it will be difficult to assuage.

Finally, you need to ascertain how relevant those differentiators are to the customers? Are they relevant and significant to them or to their area of operation? According to Elizabeth Harr, Do clients and prospects care about your differentiator? Does it resonate with them? Does it connect to that problem that keeps them up at night? Or is it just mere marketing noise? To be able to ascertain all these, as we mentioned earlier, you need to understand your clientele, their nature, their needs, and their pain points, or else what you intend to use as a differentiator may not be relevant.

Differentiation, therefore, can be looked at from two perspectives your inherent competitive advantage in the market—the things that demarcate or distinguish you from other competitors, not just in terms of your logo, brand colors, and packaging. For this to happen, there must be real differences or competitive advantages that can be used to differentiate you, your products, and brands in the market. This is becoming harder and harder to find because, except for breakthrough technology or device or approach, it is becoming difficult to find out real competitive advantages or differences that only you can lay claim to, to the exclusion of your competitors.

The second approach to differentiation, according to Elizabeth Harr, is a process that helps buyers distinguish *your* firm from similar competitors, thereby giving them a compelling reason to select you. This might involve the discovery of characteristics that your competitors have but are not emphasizing or marketing. It is akin to the discovery of a niche that is important in the minds of your consumers which no other competitor has owned, owning them and emphasizing them to such a degree that it becomes etched in the minds of your customers thereby becoming a unique identifier for your company, products or services subsequently translating into a huge selling point for you and your organization. This, according to several marketing professionals, relates to positioning what you do to the minds of your consumers or customers.

It could also be based on any of the other key aspects of the organization process like distribution, marketing, customer service, finance, etc.

At the end of the day, differentiation can be based on a tangible element or attribute or on an intangible element or property that is built into a product or service as a basis of differentiating it and making it preferred by the consumers or customers so long as it can be proved to be real or designed to become apparent.

Differentiation Strategies

Differentiation strategy, according to Hinge University, is a deliberate plan of making your firm stand out from otherwise similar competitors in the marketplace by highlighting meaningful differences between you and your competitors, which your potential clients would find valuable so as to confer or earn a competitive advantage for your firm.

Career Guide (2020) also agreed with this definition of differentiation strategy as an approach that businesses develop by providing customers with something unique, different, and distinct from items their competitors may offer in the marketplace so as to increase their competitive advantage.

There are two main approaches to differentiation strategy, which are a focused or a concentrated approach. A focused approach tries to identify and focus on a niche or narrow aspect of the market or product qualities—zeroing specifically on one or two attributes as a means of differentiating itself in the market.

A good example of a focused differentiation strategy for a company is Caterpillar. Caterpillar's focus is heavy-duty, earth-moving vehicles and equipment, such that once you hear the name Caterpillar a very clear picture of the company's product lines emerge in your thoughts, and they are usually unmistakable.

The other approach is a broad-based, more generalized approach like a basket of attributes that tries to cover a range of all the possible things that may be required by the consumers. It accommodates a larger group of attributes desired by a wider cross-section of the market. The broader reach or appeal, therefore, becomes its own basis of differentiation. A good example of this is Unilever Group, which has diversified into and has several products and brands within the various segments of the household care market ranging from soaps to lotions, food, confectionaries, etc.

Uniqueness and veracity is therefore the first test that any attribute, quality or assertion

that you want to claim about your product or services must have if not the differentiators will already be standing on shaky grounds and will not muster enough energy or force to influence or convince the customers to patronize your products.

Lorraine Carter, in her write-up, pointed out thirty different ways in which an organization can differentiate its brands using a combination of both physical characteristics of your product or services, emotional responses to brand triggers, your brand story, price points, customer experiences with your brand, its presentation, etc.

Some of the approaches to differentiating your brand as stipulated by her are as follows;

Pricing your brand differently: this involves either being the low-cost or economy bestseller within your brand segment. The idea is for you to be perceived as the best value for the bundle of offers in terms of pricing within all the different ranges of competing products available within your segment of the market. You can be perceived as the premium, high-end brand within the same segment of competing brands or as the lowest cost provider within the same range of products. These pricing strategies do not just stand alone but are supported and given credence by a lot of other tangible or perceived values by the brand. Premium brands, for instance, will come with premium high-end packaging and will be sold within premium outlets with premium displays etc. All these will combine together to give an impression of high value for the prices charged by the brand.

Mining a niche: a good example is Harley Davidson, which does not seek to cater to all motorcycle users. Their niche market, which they have successfully cultivated almost to the point of obsession for the brand, are forty-five to sixty-year-old Caucasian men and women, empty nesters with increased leisure time, who are influenced by nostalgia and a passion for recapturing their youth. They usually do not want a motorcycle for transportation but for leisure and pleasure with an aim to fulfill their dream of personal freedom. Harley Davidson has been so successful in cultivating this group to the point where they are recognized as the motorcycle brand with the highest level of loyalty amongst their customers than any other motorcycle brand with their logo ranking as the most tattooed brand in America.

Being the expert in your industry: this is a situation where the differentiation is based on some identified expertise or above-average performance on certain indices highly valued by your brand in its market segment. A good example, according to Zoovu (2017), is Canon, which has positioned itself as an expert by associating its lenses and imaging equipment with professional quality, making it abundantly clear that Canon was for people who took their pictures seriously. This has given them a 54 percent share of the world's market in DSLR cameras as of 2015, with a global market capitalization of 49.8 USD. It has also become the most successful interchangeable lens producer for 13 years in a row.

Delivering a unique point-of-purchase experience for your customers: this is usually achieved by giving your customers a good feeling about your business and nurturing customer loyalty by creating an emotional connection between your brand and your customers. A good example of a unique customer service experience is Casper, a ship to your home mattress company, which created a free chatbox for insomniacs. By simply texting "Insomnobot300" from their mobile phones, customers can talk to the chatbot about whatever is on their minds and have a real conversation. This not only helped their customers fall asleep easier but enabled them to collect mobile phone numbers for promotional offers and discounts communication. In one year, they were able to generate $100 million in sales from this approach.

Distinctive brand collaterals: a good example is Chipotle, a restaurant chain specializing in burritos, tacos, salads, etc. With only 2 percent of its revenue available for advertising, it had to embark on some innovative approaches to marketing.

One was its uniquely foil-wrapped burritos, white paper cups with brown hand lettering, which became a unique identifier and differentiator for their brand. In a bid to gain endorsements, which a lot of companies pay heavily for, they adopted a strategy of giving professional athletes who indicate their love for burritos a free burrito daily for life without asking for anything in return. A lot of these athletes eventually, in one form or other, indicate their appreciation for this gesture. These and other unique strategies earned the brand a 13.4 percent increase in store sales and a 24.4 percent increase in revenue in 2014, amounting to an amazing $904,200,000 revenue in sales in 2014.

Usage of mascots: a good example is GEICO, the American Insurance Company that has successfully differentiated itself using the talking lizard mascot. This strategy usually works when you want to introduce humor to your brand.

Heritage and provenance: this is differentiation via a close association with your country of origin or locality of production etc. A good example is whisky and red wine, where the location of production or plantation of the grapes is a prominent means of differentiation, e.g., Scotch Whisky—specifically for whisky produced in Scotland, Irish whisky, Japanese whisky, Bourbon whisky, which is specifically American, etc. Another good example is Danish milk, ice creams, chocolates, etc.

Innovation is also another good means of differentiation: a good example has been Diageo which has remarkable been known to innovate different kinds of drink brands like the ready-to-drink brands Smirnoff Ice, Bacardi Breezer, Vodka Cruiser, etc. Patagonia, another highly innovative brand, ranked topmost among the first-timers in the Brand Keys annual survey of innovative brands in 2019. This it was able to achieve through its ability to authentically tie a meaningful cause to its business and help people connect to their desires to be better humans.

Renaming an already existing product might be a wonderful way of differentiating it in the market and giving the customers the impression of novelty arising from a new product. Innumerable examples abound of such successful name changes that reversed the fortune of the brand and effectively differentiated it in the market. A good example is Anderson consulting, which after the infamous Enron crisis, changed its name to Accenture. AT&T Broadband changed its name to Comcast in 2002; Bank America card service became Visa in 1970; Blackrub became Google in 1996; Burbn—Instagram; Brad's drink—Pepsi; Pete's Super Submarines—Subway; Blue Ribbon Sports—Nike; Cadabra—Amazon; Tokyo Tsushi Kogya—Sony; Cargo House—Starbucks; AuctionWeb—eBay; Computing Tabulating Recording Corporation—IBM; Phoenix—Firefox; David's and Jerry's Guide to the World Wide Web—Yahoo; Sky Peer to Peer—Skype and other innumerable successful examples. By simply changing the name of the brand, you attract a different mindset, attitude, and connotation to the brand, which can be an essential ingredient in its success.

Being the underdog or the fighter or activist brand: customers are always in love with good start-up stories taking on the establishment and will most likely pitch their support and emotions with the underdog. One reason for the huge success of Patagonia has been its crusading and activist spirit in seeking to preserve the environment. It led over forty firms in giving a work-free day to their employees to vote. Richard Branson and his Virgin brand exploit this approach in all the sectors they have ventured into, Virgin Cola, Virgin Air, Virgin Music, etc.

Convenience has also been a huge differentiator in any business, but the problem is that standing alone, it is easily copied like the bank ATM, which has become commoditized, drive-through services in fast food restaurants. However, organizations like Amazon have been able to differentiate themselves effectively via this approach because of the wide variety of services that it offers; books, different kinds of consumer goods, financing, etc. Very few if any other establishment can effectively set up to compete on all these parameters alongside Amazon.

Exceptional customer service can also be a means of differentiating both a brand and an organization. This involves an unconditional commitment to giving the highest level of product or service to every person, regardless of the circumstances. Examples of such exceptional and consistent customer service abound, like Ritz-Carlton hotels where there is such a strong emotional engagement between the hotels' staff and their guests that a guest will not consider staying anywhere else, even if they have an option. A good example of such exceptional customer service is the story where the hotel had to fly someone 1,680 kilometers in a two-hour-and-forty-five-minute flight from Bali in Indonesia to Singapore just to deliver a specialty egg and milk from a store there to the child of a guest who has some allergies—all at no cost to the guest.

Extraordinary, out-of-the-box packaging: most brands within the same market segment follow similar designs or shapes in their packaging, with only the color and the company logo being the differentiator. The emphasis most of the time is often on maximizing space at the shelf within the outlets. The brand that usually blazes the trail in tweaking or coming up with different packaging or design has a lot of room in differentiating itself in the market. Not only will it be different from all the other brands but also it will attract more attention and customers sometimes out of curiosity will want to try out this new and different product brand. This is why year in year out car manufacturers fall over themselves in coming up with new designs for their cars. Usually, the car with the more pleasurable or distinct designs carries the day because the engine capacity and performance of each range of these cars are usually well known to the customers.

The problem you solve or seek to solve can be a great differentiator for your brand. Every brand seeks to solve a problem, but some problems are more visible or significant and consequently elicit a wide range of support from critical sections of the public. A good example is TOM shoes which, by seeking to solve the problem of lack of shoes among the world's poor population through donating one shoe for every shoe bought, galvanized the public and differentiated their brand. It also created a huge emotional connection between the customers and the brand.

Brand story as a differentiator: every brand has its own unique brand story that can be used to create emotional bonding with the customers but how well it serves as a lasting differentiator is suspect. This is because as good as your brand story is, it is in the past and how long it can continue to inspire or serve as a differentiator is not known. Coca-Cola, as a brand with an origin in the eighteenth century, cannot continually depend on its brand story as a major differentiator for the brand. Once you have heard it with its inspiring nature, for how long it can continue to serve as an inspiration and a credible differentiator between it and other brands is highly suspect. The brand has to continuously seek other grounds of differentiation other than the initial differentiating effect created by its brand story.

Be relevantly shocking: this strategy appropriately suits the one adopted by Prince, the legendary musician, in launching himself to fame. This involves going against the grain or adopting a different route other than that adopted by every other brand. This strategy can only work if it is aptly supported by a gilt-edge performance by the brand. If the brand is mediocre or a non-performer, this strategy will amount to a complete turn-off and an irritating factor. But if supported by above-average performance, it will be considered as one of the idiosyncrasies or nuances of the brand, which can be tolerated. If these shocking behaviors of the brand are tied to a good cause that further sensitizes the customers to a worthy cause that might have been overlooked, the better for the brand. In that case, it will be seen as a crusading aspect of the brand.

Change your customer experience: every brand segment, market, or industry is known for a particular set of similar customer service experiences created for their customers. Breaking away from this set of similar customer service experiences and setting up a new one will be a wonderful way of differentiating your brand and your organization. A good example is Apple, which changed the concept of their Apple store experience for their customers. They created a concept that changed the retail landscape forever at a time when a lot of other manufacturers were closing their retail outlets. They stopped selling their products through third-party stores and created a store where they can engage with the customers (where the customers can freely interface with their brands unhindered), convey a clear message about the brand, and create a venue with superior visual articulation. They built an environment designed entirely around the consumer, where service, learning, and products were combined. People were allowed to try out and learn about the products, as well as ask questions at the Genius Bar, an idea similar to concierge service at a nice hotel. The concept is to develop a store that doesn't necessarily need to sell, but a store as a place where you activate your brand, where you show what the brand stands for. Despite this, the store sells approximately $5,546 per square foot, the highest among all retail stores.

Personalizing the brand: research from Salesforce.com shows that 75 percent of business buyers expect the companies they buy from to provide personalized experiences, anticipate their individual needs, and provide relevant suggestions (Brooks, 2020). Allowing your customers the ownership of your brand through interactive buying experiences can form a basis for differentiating your brand in the market. A good example is the Share a Coke campaign that was targeted at reconnecting with the young adults and the teen market. Research showed that 50 percent of this group had not enjoyed a Coca-Cola in the last month. The campaign, which started in Australia, printed the 150 most popular Australian names on Coke bottles and cans and invited Australians to "Share a Coke." The rest is history. The campaign ran in over eighty markets over a seven-year period, featuring popular names in countries from Australia to Vietnam. The campaign reversed an eleven-year consumption decline in the US and helped the drinks brand boost its presence across international markets.

Link your brand to an occasion, and own it: this is important such that once the event is being thought about, your brand will also be mentioned or in the picture. Some good examples are Coca-Cola and the World Cup. For many years now, Coca-Cola has been identified with the World Cup, not just the sponsorship. They make out time and funds to fly the world cup across the world for viewing and photo opportunities by major stakeholders and citizens of these countries amidst heavy publicity. Another good example is Guinness and St Patrick's Day in Ireland, which is like a national holiday and a huge day of festivities. This also celebrates the heritage of the brand with Ireland, its country of origin.

Personification of your brand is also another means of differentiating it from other brands. Personification, according to Mktresearch.org, is a projective technique that asks people to think about brands as if they were people and to describe how the brands would think or feel. It also involves the giving of an object or animal characteristics to a brand so as to create interesting imagery. It usually makes it easier for consumers to connect with a personality than with a handful of claims or benefits. A very good example was Marlboro using the Marlboro country and the Marlboro man, the cowboy, which has been one of the most enduring images for the brand.

Repositioning your category by changing what the customers think, associate, or expect from your brand category is another way of differentiating your brand. This can involve changing your messaging, the personality of the brand (Pork to lean meat), your product offerings with respect to the features of the brand or its competitors, the brand's promise, brand essence, etc. A good example of this is Starbucks, which repositioned the entire coffee market or business. Coffee was positioned as something you don't just buy and go but as something you really relish and Starbucks as the third place from home and work where you can go relax, unwind and catch up on life, listen to music while drinking your favorite personalized coffee, baked pastries with a free Wi-Fi, etc. to enable you to browse and possibly catch up on your work or hobbies.

Importance/ Benefits of Differentiation

Differentiation is one of the few remaining barriers to competition in the industry. Technology and innovations have been democratized such that they offer very few advantages, especially as what is available to A is also available to B. With the effect that once you can afford it, then there will be uniformity in the production process.

It also acts as a major deterrent to the copying or imitation of your product or services. Your differentiation feeds into your design, branding, and packaging as well as communication, thereby solidifying and accentuating your brand positioning.

Differentiation is a principal key in building strong brands because the more differentiated your brands are in the market, the more memorable and satisfying they will be for your customers. This satisfaction will also lead to more repeat customers and purchases.

The more differentiated your brands are, the higher the price points that it can attract, mainly due to the additional benefits of durability, class, privilege, as well as the benefit of being associated with your brand that the customers will gain. Examples of such abound in the auto industry like Lamborghini etc.

Differentiation is an effective tool for profiling your customers, producing exclusive products for specific customer groups, partnering with them, giving them what they want, thereby deepening your share of their wallet, and growing your business with a captive customer group.

Differentiation, according to Sharp and Dawes, provides a firm with something of a "mini" or weak monopoly, since no other product or services can lay claim to the same things offered by the differentiated product, nor can any other product or brand fill the same void in the absence of the brand.

Differentiation makes the brand an imperfect substitute with other brands, so buyers of the brand are more loyal, and therefore its customer base is more secure. This makes the brand less susceptible to the activity of competitor brands.

Differentiation, Distinctiveness, and Salience
Romaniuk, Sharp and Ehrenberg argue that differentiation plays a more limited role in brand competition than the orthodox literature assumes, mainly because there is a low level of perceived differentiation across competing brands. According to them, if brand-level differentiation exists, whereby a brand appeals to a defined customer base that particularly values the differentiated feature, then we might expect many brands to differ in terms of the types of customers they attract. Yet brand user-profiles rarely differ greatly in demographics or other customer identifying variables (Kennedy and Ehrenberg, 2001; Kennedy et al., 2000).

Brands of vastly different prices and quality do have different user profiles. Expensive brands tend to be bought by wealthier people—but within their competitive set, the brands' user bases look similar. Versace's buyers are similar to those of Gucci. Ultimately, competitive brands all appeal to similar types of customers; some brands just have more buyers than others.

It will be very interesting to probe further if actually the buyers of Gucci and Versace, BMW and Mercedes, are exactly alike in terms of their profiles. Other than demographics, can they also be said to be the same in terms of psychographics? Also, are there not basic differences in these brands that can appeal to one group of people and repel the other. Is Gucci the same in terms of brand perceived difference with Versace? Are the two brands appealing to the same customer groups? Do Versace customers see themselves as the same as Gucci and vice versa?

To explain why customers still buy or prefer one brand to another despite this lack of perceived and valued differentiation according to them, they placed emphasis on distinctiveness instead of differentiation as the epicenter of brand strategy. This, according to them, is the point where a brand builds unique associations that makes it more easily identifiable. The issue then becomes, are these unique associations not basic elements of differentiation? Differentiation does not have to lie within the product brand itself but can as well lies in these unique associations created by the brand.

For these unique associations to function as instruments of easier identification, then they point to or are indicative of cherished values and positions to the consumers of the brand. These unique identifiers or associations definitely appeal to specific customer groups and not to all customers; hence it serves as a basis of differentiation. For it to appeal to some and not all customer, therefore, presupposes that the customers are also in some basic forms different from one another even if they share some similarities in their profile.

According to (Ehrenberg et al., 2004), if differentiation theory works the way it has been stipulated, then we should expect a great deal of market partitioning, where brands share more or fewer customers than would be expected based on their respective market shares. Yet the widespread fit of the "Duplication of Purchase law" which states that brands share customers with other brands in line with their relative shares, shows that partitioning is generally fairly rare and often small (Ehrenberg et al., 2004).

Consequently, brands that appear close together on a perceptual map do share customers more than brands that are positioned further apart, but this is not the case. Instead, it appears that image positions are largely independent of brand buying patterns (Sharp et al., 2003; Sharp and Sharp, 1997).

In continuation of their arguments, they posited that there is sufficient situation-level differentiation in marketplaces for choice to take place (and preferences exist) without buyers perceiving brand-level differentiation (Sharp and Dawes, 2001). The result, therefore, is that most buyers of a brand do not see it as ***different or unique***. Yet, they still buy them.

This behavior for them is a result of two factors the distinctive nature of the brand as well as its salience.

Distinctive qualities of the brand, according to them, are the other elements of the brand identity that can substitute for the brand name and helps the consumer to notice, recognize and recall the brand in buying situations and/or when the brand is advertising, as they provide additional stimuli for processing. These elements can include colors such as the Coca-Cola red, logos such as the McDonald's arches, taglines such as Nike's "just do it," symbols/characters such as Mickey Mouse's ears, celebrities such as Tiger Woods for Nike, and advertising styles like MasterCard's "priceless" campaign.

It is also anything that communicates the brand name at the most basic level, which can be used in packaging, advertising, in-store displays, and sponsorships –any activity where the marketer wants the consumer to identify the brand. The aim of which is to create, refresh or reinforce consumer memory structures in order to build consumer-based brand equity (Aaker, 1996; Keller, 2003) or to facilitate actual purchase by making the brand easier to locate. The stronger/fresher these distinctive qualities and the more link in memory, the easier it is for the consumer to identify the brand.

If the only differences that buyers see in the brands are the brand colors, logos, taglines, etc., and nothing unique or different in the actual brand offerings, then there is a big problem. For example, if all the differences existing between Nike and Addidas or that buyers see is their logo, colors, advertising styles, etc., then a great injustice and abnormality would have been meted out to the brands because, in actual fact, factual differences exist between the various brands. The implication of this is also that all you need to market your brand or gain market share will be to specialize in all these ephemerals as opposed to the tangibles. As effective as these distinctive factors are, experience has also shown that using different competing brands will throw up their basic differences and consumers who have used the two will tell you about these basic differences. Just like the blind test between Coca-Cola and Pepsi has consistently shown a preference in over 60 percent of the time for Pepsi as opposed to Coca-Cola.

Having an easily identifiable brand, according to Ehrenberg et al., 2004 also reduces the risk in message strategy. It lets a brand communicate a message or value proposition that is highly relevant to consumers but not unique. This means marketers can concentrate on refreshing and reminding consumers of core messages, rather than constantly searching for new unique points of difference that risk focusing on areas of little value to the consumer (Keller et al., 2002).

According to Sharp and Dawes, purchase preference certainly exists, but it is often a function of *salience* (each buyer knows some brands better than others), *habit* ("this is the one we usually buy") and/or *availability* ("this one has my size"), rather than product differences between the brands. This knowledge of some brands better than others could also have arisen as a result of an experience in using the brand and being satisfied with it such that there is no need to further search or keep searching for alternatives. This knowledge or habit may have also arisen from having tried a couple of brands in the market and finally settling for the one that best meets the needs of the consumer. In other words, habit and knowledge do not just arise. They are predicated on experience or the previous usage of the brand and possibly other competing brands.

According to Sharp and Dawes, differences in customer awareness, brand familiarity, knowledge of product features, situational factors, and distribution all combine with habits (e.g., brand loyalty) and variety seeking to produce brand preferences.

In concluding their paper, they agreed that brands typically enjoy some differentiation, usually from things other than product feature differences, but this differentiation is more a market feature than a brand-specific feature.

Their view of differentiation is one that is about making the offer different in response to differences in demand (demand heterogeneity), which can be achieved through altering any aspect of the offering (not just product features), including the financial cost of acquisition (i.e., the price charged).

 At the end of the day, that differentiation is one of the major planks of brand strategy is not in doubt what is the subject of discussion is how to achieve that differentiation either through brand differences engineered into the product or a situation where a brand builds unique associations that makes it more easily identifiable and subsequently preferred in the market place.

Interestingly also, Ehrenberg et al. acknowledged the role that design has played in the differentiation and preferences of certain brands like Roll Royce, etc., and were of the opinion that this should be further studied. At the end of the day, it is not an either-or situation, but a conscious and deliberate focus on wherever competitive advantage or stronger value proposition lies for the brand for it to fully exploit it so as to derive the maximum benefit from it in differentiating and positioning its brands.

Tim Calkins (2005) summarized it effectively in his work by stating that brands function as a prism and how people regard a branded product is shaped by both the actual product; its specific features and attributes and by the brand, not any one of them singly but a combination of all these elements.

CHAPTER SEVEN

Brand Positioning

The bitter truth, according to Philip Kotler, is that traditional marketing is no longer working or effective in the present world of hyper-competition, commoditization, globalization, and rapid technological obsolescence hence the concerted efforts by marketers to develop new concepts and paradigms that will enable them design and deliver their marketing programs successfully.

According to him, mass advertising campaigns are money losers; sales promotion campaigns only boost sales temporarily despite being unprofitable, while new products are failing at unprecedented rates with direct mailing campaigns barely able to deliver a 1 percent response rate. The only option open to marketers are either to get closer to their customers and know them better or to differentiate their offering through branding to the extent that it stands out as relevant and superior in value to the target market.

Branding, according to him, is much more than attaching a name to an offering but is about making a certain promise to customers about delivering a fulfilling experience and a level of performance. Branding, therefore, becomes the central platform for planning, designing, and delivering superior value to the company's target customers, with everyone within the supply chain working toward the actualization of this promise.

The brand transcends the product. Harley Davidson, for instance, is not unique only because it makes good motorcycles; there are many other companies across the world that make good motorcycles too. Harley Davidson is unique because it has a powerful brand that connects with its customers (Tim Calkins, 2005).

Having a clear positioning for your brand is a good start but not all that is required in building a very strong brand. In addition to good positioning, brands also need to be creative in the market to attract attention. Marketers must identify and execute creative ideas that are unique and attract attention. A good example is Red Bull's strategy of sponsorship for extreme, high-energy sports.

Brand positioning is a corollary of the USP (unique selling point) propounded by Rosser Reeves in the 1950s. According to Rosser Reeves, the uniqueness of every product (their rational appeal - benefits, attributes, and features) should be highlighted in the marketplace and should be constantly bombarded in the minds of the consumer to the point where they become entrenched in their minds. The only problem, however, is that these USPs can be easily copied by the competitors.

Al Ries and Jack Trout, in the early 1980s, as a result of the onslaught of competition from Japanese manufacturers, coined the term "positioning," which they argued is not what you do to the product but what you do to the minds of the consumers.

Positioning enlarged the appeals developed by Rosser Reeves from benefits, attributes, and features to encompass the emotional appeals, all aimed at differentiating the brand from the competition and building an emotional bond with the consumer in their hearts and mind.

Product/Brand Positioning

It is important to point out ab initio that a brand's positioning is not a clever advertising idea, a catchy tag line, a slick logo, a graphic standard, directions or manual, or a website. As important as all these are, they are just tools that combine together to accentuate or drive home a brand's positioning. The brand's positioning is the foundation from where all these spring from or the objective that all these tools aim to actualize or bring about; the strategic thread that weaves all of them into a cohesive and coherent entity.

Brand positioning is a strategic and systematic process of setting your business or brands apart from the rest by making it occupy a prime position in your customer's heart and mind. It can also be looked upon as the size or proportion of space that your brand occupies or owns in the minds of your customers with regards to the product category or class in which you operate.

Positioning provides the link between the internal analysis and the external competitive environment of the firm. Interestingly according to Ostaseviciute and Sliburyte, there is no product in the world that does not have a position because the product's positioning refers to the visibility and recognition of a product and what it represents for a buyer.

The whole idea behind product positioning, according to Boone and Kurz (2001), is that there is a certain position that the owners of the product want the product to occupy in the minds of the prospective buyers or customers. For a product to be successful, therefore, it must occupy an explicit, distinct, and proper place in the minds of potential and existing consumers relative to other rival products in the market.

Trout (2012) identifies positioning as encompassing a body of work on how the mind works in the process of communication, a conception that characterizes positioning as a battle for the mind (Ries & Trout, 1986).

Product positioning is therefore very important for the customers in that it assists them in their buying decisions. Owing to the huge number of decisions that customers make on a regular basis in evaluating or choosing products to buy, they develop or create compartments in their minds where they store product decisions and comparative variables such that at moments of decision-making, fresh evaluations are not started all over again, but the stored results about the various product groups are retrieved to facilitate decision making at that point.

Buyers, therefore, group or position products in their minds in their rank orders or preference ratios. The challenge of the marketer is, therefore, to ensure that his products become the benchmark of evaluations or occupy the prime positions in the evaluation process such that his products form the reference point for the products within that product category with which all other products are measured or evaluated with. Some brands have come to represent their entire product categories like Coke for soda or carbonated soft drinks; Kleenex for tissue papers; 3M post it for stick-up notes etc.

The bitter truth according to Philip Kotler is that traditional marketing is no longer working or effective in the present world of hyper competition, commoditization, globalization and rapid technological obsolescence hence

According to Branding News, brand positioning is the union between segmentation and differentiation. In other words: successfully positioning a brand will result in the brand occupying a differentiated position at the head of a specific market segment; if the company does not offer something different, consumers see no reason why they should not opt for what the competition offers.

Tybout and Sternthal (2005) defined brand positioning as the specific intended meaning for the brand in the consumers' minds. It articulates the goal that a consumer will achieve by using the brand and explains why it is superior to other means of accomplishing this goal. This is definitely one sure way to break away from the clutter and heavy advertising campaigns and hyper-competition in the market that seeks to inundate the consumer with different kinds of information about different brands.

In cutting through the clutters in the market, positioning helps the brand/ product to reach the desired place in the minds and hearts of the customer. The ability to reach (or not reach) the desired position in the minds of consumers is the result of a successful (or not successful) positioning strategy.

It is, however, important to point out that there are only specific combinations of the marketing mix elements that can support or uphold a particular positioning that a product chooses. In other words, there is only a specific marketing mix that will influence or reinforce the customer's perception of a product or brand in line with its chosen positioning. So the product's positioning will determine the kind of marketing mix that will be deployed to achieve the particular positioning objective (Lamb, Hair & McDaniel, 2004).

Great brands, according to Tim Calkins, mean something unique and distinct for customers and also have a very clear set of associations. Weak brands, on the other hand, are bland and do not stand for anything in particular and consequently mean nothing. They also struggle because they have no focus and do not stand out. For example, Walmart stands for low prices; Tiffany is synonymous with luxury and exclusivity; Viagra is about erectile dysfunction, whereas Red Bull stands for energy and excitement.

David Aaker, in his own work, weighed in strongly on the association dimension of positioning. According to him, positioning is closely related to the association and image concepts only that it implies or exists within a frame of reference, the reference point usually being competition. This association or image, according to him, is defined in the context of an attribute—friendliness, size, competence, etc., in relation of the brand to another competitor. A well-positioned brand will therefore have a competitively attractive position, which is supported by strong associations, a desirable attribute where it rates very highly on or even occupies a position distinct from that of competitors. At the end of the day, a brand position does not only reflect how the brand is currently being perceived but also how the brand wants itself to be perceived.

Brand positioning, according to Jean Kapferer, is, therefore, the emphasizing of the distinctive characteristics that make the brand different from its competitors and appealing to the public.

Brand positioning is also a process of establishing and managing the images, perceptions, and associations that the consumer applies to your product based on the values and beliefs associated with your product. Brand positioning, therefore, shares some similarities with the brand image construct, which according to Fuchs and Diamantopoulos, is "the concept of a brand that is held by the consumer, a largely subjective and perceptual phenomenon that is formed through consumer interpretation, whether reasoned or emotional." The major difference between brand image and brand positioning is that brand positioning uses an explicit frame of reference, usually the competition in arriving at its position.

Brand positioning can therefore be summarized as the strategic and systematic process of setting your business or brands apart from the rest by making it occupy a prime position in your customer's heart and mind as well as a differentiated position at the head of a specific market segment.

It is also the specific intended meaning for the brand in consumers' minds that is closely related to the association and image concepts of the brand within its frame of reference.

The end result of positioning, according to Kotler, is the successful creation of a customer-focused value proposition, a cogent reason why the target market should buy the product."

To arrive at a brand's positioning is not the outcome or product of guesswork, but according to Kapferer, the outcome of an analytical process based on the answers to four questions;

- A brand for what benefit? Which is a direct allusion to the brand's promise and consumer benefit or the target's goal that can be achieved by the consumption of the brand. This goal or frame of reference then becomes a guide for the selection of the target market, the situation in which the brand can be used as well as in the definition of competitors.

- A brand for whom? A reference to the specific target audience or customer base for the brand, which it is being positioned for, which according to Tybout and Sternthal, includes the demographics and psychographics (activities, interests, and opinions) of the target group.

- Reason; the factual or subjective elements that support the claimed benefits, which according to Tybout and Sternthal, are the reasons to believe. This, according to them, is usually preceded by an assertion or allusion to the reasons why the brand is regarded as being superior to other brands or alternatives in the frame of reference, which is known as the points of difference.

- A brand against whom? This refers to the competitive set or context for the brand or, in other words, the main competitors that can be targeted and possibly captured by the brand.

Winner (2007), in his position, which is more like a further elaboration or addition to Kapferer's position, emphasized the importance of the customer decision-making process as the most important issue in product positioning. He added four more questions to make the previous questions by Kapferer more robust.

For instance, he wanted to find out;

- What dimensions do consumers use to evaluate product offerings in the industry or category? In evaluating fast-food restaurants, for instance, what are the parameters that consumers use in evaluating each of the fast-food restaurants. Mcdonald's discovered this quite early (quality, cleanliness, service, and value) and capitalized on it in their positioning.

- How important is each of these dimensions in the decision-making process? All these parameters though important, do not have equal weightings. For instance, if the environment is not clean, no matter how good the food is, most people will not venture in there.

- How do you and competition compare on these dimensions?

- What decision processes do the customers use? E.g., in the decision-making process about which fast food restaurant to patronize, whose decision in the family weighs most or who is given the highest consideration in such decisions?

Brand Positioning Map

Positioning map is an important tool in the development and tracking of promotional strategy. It enables managers to identify gaps and opportunities in the market and allows monitoring of the effects of past marketing communications (Arora, 2006).

Positioning map, according to Ostaseviciute and Sliburyte (2008), provides a valuable means in trying to position a product by graphically illustrating consumers' perceptions of competing products and the product being positioned.

A competitive positioning map can always be created from information obtained from surveying the consumers. Different attributes, e.g., price and perceived quality, benefits, users, etc., can be put together to find out how the product is rated viz-a-viz competing products.

According to Arora (2006), the positioning map develops an understanding of how the relative strengths and weaknesses of different products are perceived by buyers. It also builds knowledge about the similarities and dissimilarities between competing products.

It ensures that the positioning exercise is not based on the figment of the imagination of the marketers but based on empirical evidence that can be evaluated.

It helps in the tracking of the perception that buyers have of a particular product as well as in the measurement of the effectiveness of the communication programs and marketing activities aimed at changing the perceptions of the buyers over time.
It is also a good tool in the formulation and tracking of promotional strategies as it helps the marketers identify gaps and opportunities in the market that can be filled or exploited with the various promotional and marketing mix strategies.

Brand Positioning Strategies
According to Fuchs and Diamantopoulos, the decision to select the most effective positioning strategy constitutes the main challenge for marketers since it is central to consumers' perceptions and choices (Aaker and Shansby, 1982). If positioning is done effectively, it has the potential to build powerful brands; however, if done incorrectly, it can also result in disaster. The real challenge in formulating positioning strategies is, therefore, to ensure that it resonates with your target audience and also that it leads to tangible business results.
Just like in so many other areas of life, emphasis may not have been deliberately placed on trying to determine the most salient and beneficial positioning for the product or brand. A lot of manufac-

turers focus their attention only on production and sales with the erroneous notion that good products will always sell themselves, thereby losing a lot of advantages and benefits that proper positioning of their product will offer to them.

To be successful, therefore, marketers have to deliberately plan, choose and pursue positions that distinguish their products from competing products which will also give them the greatest strategic advantage in their target markets (Ostaseviciute & Sliburyte, 2008).

For Fuchs and Diamantopoulos, the concept of positioning effectiveness is a multidimensional construct that captures the consumers' evaluations of a brand's position in terms of credible and favorable differentiation in relation to competing brands, thus enabling an assessment of the extent to which the brand in question occupies a credible, distinct, and positively valued position in the minds of consumers.

For them, there is also a difference between strategic (market) positioning and brand (operational) positioning. Strategic (market) positioning refers to the competitive market standing of a firm against its competitors, a situation whereby firms seek to find ways of deploying firm-specific resources and assets to build positional advantages in product markets, whereas brand (operational) positioning focuses on (the process of creating and altering) perceptions of consumers about a firm's products or brands.

The strategic (market) positioning, according to them, sets the pace and direction for the brand (operational) positioning. For instance, if a company intends to become the technology leader in a product category, it needs to develop the skills or allocate resources to achieve this position (for example, through high R&D investments or other initiatives). This is the strategic (market) positioning decision that it needs to make for the brand to ride on its back to position itself as the leading edge brand within its competitive frame of reference.

To appreciate the strategic (market) positioning, it is important to note that the same way products have a position in the market, the organization itself also has a position both in the market and in the minds of the customers. What is therefore important, according to Adokou and Kyere—Diabour, is for an organization, product, or brand to have a distinct position with which it is able to convey to prospective customers what it is and what it stands for through its marketing activities and to also occupy a prime position in the minds of consumers, as well as create a specific and harmonious image about itself.

Positioning strategy, according to Doyle (1983), is the choice of target market segment, which describes the customers a business will seek to serve and the choice of differential advantage that defines how it will compete with rivals in that segment.

The positioning strategy, therefore, stands on the tripod of three key elements: the customer target, the competitive target, and the principle of competitive advantage, which in other words represents the STP (segmentation, targeting, and positioning) principle of marketing.

In talking about the competitive advantage, it is also very important for the organization to understand where their business fits in the market, vis-a`-vis the competition. Without this knowledge, it will be very difficult to identify a differential advantage for the organization or its brands that will give it the necessary competitive edge to attract the target customer. For example, if Toyota does not know clearly where it stands or fits in the market as a company, it will be difficult for it to position its brands creditably in the market.

Two sets of variables, according to Mckechnie et al., are essential in categorizing the position held by any business; (its strategic market positioning); first, does the business or competitor operate with a company-focused philosophy, or is it competition-focused? Second, does the business or competitor push the competitive boundaries of business or stay within boundaries?

A business in the leadership role, according to them, will be company-focused to defend its position and market share while pushing the boundaries to expand the market. The challenger is competition-focused, as in "watching what the leader does" while maintaining a course of action that also pushes boundaries in the marketplace. The follower follows. The follower will watch the leader and challenger and, in some instances, attempt to imitate or copy their actions.

Generally, however, the follower stays the safe course within boundaries. The business in the niche position knows its own strengths and weaknesses vis-a`-vis the major competition and stays focused on its own business endeavors. It can be a leading edge within its own parameters yet does not push the boundaries in the larger market environment.

For the organization or its brands, there are only four possible positions that it can possibly occupy in the market; that of a leader, challenger, follower, or niche follower. These positions are important also because they are indicative of the level of resources available to the firm or brand to pursue and sustain its desired positioning in the market.

The positioning strategy helps the organization to achieve positioning advantage based on their understanding and ability to satisfy distinct consumer needs (Lovelock and Wirtz, 2011; Coffie, 2016). The positioning strategy also helps in highlighting the product's intrinsic values, which separates or distinguishes it from all other products within the same product category.

Prominent product positioning strategies recommended by several marketing researchers are product features, price/quality, product class dissociation, user, competition, benefit, heritage, or cultural symbols (Fill 2006, Kotler 2007, Armstrong 2004, and Doyle 2006). Other researchers like Boone and Kurz (2001) in their own paper included other positioning strategies like attributes, competitors, product users, product class and applications, etc.

According to Lefkoff-Hagius and Mason, 1993; Sirgy, 1982, the user positioning strategy provides favorability by associating consumers with their desired or actual membership group, role, or self-image, which in turn satisfies their need for self-expression or social approval. This positioning strategy, according to Fuchs and Diamantopoulos, is usually much harder to be duplicated.

Blankson and Kalafatis (2000), in their own paper, outlined eight other positioning strategies;

- Top of the range refers to a positioning strategy alluding to being upper class, with a focus on status, prestige, and being posh.

- Service, a focus on delivering impressive, gilt-edge service, personal attention, treating people as important and friendly service.

- Value for money—based on affordability, reasonable service, and value for money.

- Reliability is based on the durability of the product, warranty, safety, reliability, and the general quality of the product.

- Attractiveness hinged on good aesthetics, attractive, cool, elegant ambiance, especially with regards to the environment or packaging.

- Country of origin—patriotism, country of origin, and association with what the countries are prominent for

- Branding—the brand name, leaders in the market, extra features, choice, wide range, premium quality.

- Selectivity—discriminatory in the selection of customers, selective in the choice of customers, high principle or exquisite.

It can safely be alluded to that the positioning strategies outlined by the various researchers above follow the product/service divide. The positioning strategies of Blankson and Kalafatis (2004) have the service-based organizations in mind while that enunciated by Fill 2006, Kotler 2007, Armstrong 2004, and Doyle 2006, Boone and Kurz are more amenable to product-based brands and organizations.

An Explanation of the Different Types of Positioning Strategies

Product attribute positioning strategy, according to David Aaker, is when you associate an object with a product attribute or characteristics. This can translate to reasons to buy, especially when the attribute is meaningful or significant or vis versa. A good example is Crest, with its strong association with cavity control or Sensodyne with tooth sensitivity.

The key to product attribute positioning is an attribute that is important to a major segment of the market, which has not been claimed by the competitor, and to focus and capitalize on that. The temptation, according to Aaker, also lies in trying to associate a brand with so many attributes in a bid to cover or take care of every possible selling argument or segment of the market. Attempting to actualize this will be the easiest and shortest shortcut to a confusing product positioning as not only will the positioning end up being clouded but also contradictory. A single-minded proposition is usually more effective, easier to process for the consumers, and much more believable.

Owing to the never-ending competition and communication assertion by different firms to being better, more reliable, faster, and more effective across so many parameters and dimensions, consumers after a while lose confidence or trust in all those claims as the basis of substantiating them keeps getting eroded or becoming thinner and thinner with each new or subsequent innovation. For instance, on what major parameters of believability can the different manufacturers of airplanes use in substantiating their claims of being better or faster than their competitors?

Product owners, in a bid to avoid this rut, often detour and make use of Intangible product positioning strategies. This, according to Aaker, refers to general attributes such as perceived quality, technological leadership, perceived value, etc., which serve to summarize sets of more objective attributes. A good example is Apple, which has been able to position itself as a premium brand that is highly loved by people. People stay for weeks in a queue waiting for the release of the latest Apple products. Apple was able to position itself effectively in the market while focusing on these key tenets and values of simplicity, creativity, Innovation, imagination, humanity, and design.

Such intangible attributes like simplicity, user-friendliness, creativity, design, just like technology, health, or nutrition, are more difficult to imitate or copy as opposed to tangible product attributes like the speed of the microprocessor etc., which can always be improved upon or made better by another competitor.

Customer benefits refer to a good or helpful result or effects that are realized from the brand as opposed to the physical characteristics, features, or attributes of the brand. These benefits, according to (Sengupta, 2005), are more relevant to the consumer's evaluation of the brand than the physical characteristics or attributes of the brand because they are actually intended to solve a need or a problem.

The demarcating point in the product attributes or benefit positioning for the customer, according to Aaker, is when the brand comes to mind or is mentioned, does the customer think about the ingredients or components of the product, or how the brand makes him feel. When you talk about BMW, is it the horsepower of the engine that comes to mind or the pleasurable driving experience that the brand offers that comes to the consumer's mind?

To be successful therefore marketers have to deliberately plan, choose and pursue positions that distinguish their products from competing products that will also give them the greatest strategic advantage in their target markets (Ostaseviciute & Sliburyte, 2008).

Product benefits are often considered a superior form of product positioning because consumers buy a product because of the benefits derivable from them and not necessarily because of the features or characteristics of these products. Sometimes also, product owners often attribute characteristics and features to their products that are meaningless or of no major impact to the consumers. Most times also, the product category is filled with almost identical and common features that do not have much impact on the consumers' choice or selection process. For example, cars are categorized as eight or six cylinders, which to the average customer does not mean much. All cars presently do have ABS, which in terms of actually positioning the cars may not mean much except if tied to a greater benefit accruable to the consumer.

Benefit positioning, according to Fuchs and Diamantopoulos, can be further subdivided into direct (functional) benefit positioning and indirect (experiential/symbolic) benefit positioning. Direct benefit positioning refers to the communication of the intrinsic advantage of using or possessing the brand and is primarily derived from brand features that tend to be functional in nature. Indirect benefits, on the other hand, are conceptualized as "follow-on" results from direct benefits and tend to satisfy experiential (i.e., sensory pleasure, fun, excitement, cognitive stimulation, etc.) or symbolic (i.e., self-fulfillment, social acceptance and approval, self-esteem, etc.) needs.

Indirect benefit positioning is, therefore, more useful for hedonic goods (e.g., designer clothes, luxury watches, sports cars, etc.), which base their superiority on fun, pleasure, and excitement. For utilitarian product categories (e.g., alkaline batteries, vacuum cleaners, computers, etc.), direct benefit positioning, which creates primarily functional performance-related associations, will be more aligned to the consumers' needs (utilitarian) and, therefore, also more effective than indirect (experiential/ symbolic) positioning.

Relative price positioning refers to a positioning strategy that capitalizes on one of the five major price bands for most products or consumer items while trying to make it stand apart from other products within the same price band by trying to relate it to the product offering a higher price level.

The main price bands, according to David Aker, are the prestige price range, which ranks highest within the price ranges and quite above the super-premium category. This is followed by the economy price band, the lower price band, and the lowest end of the price range that is represented by the store or discount brands. This positioning strategy can also backfire if not well handled, thereby leading to a confused positioning where the positioning strategy conflicts with the already existing image about the product or brand in the minds of the consumers.

Use—Application by Customers

This positioning strategy aims at associating a brand with use or application. A good example, according to David Aaker, is the nine identified user occasions for coffee; to start the day, between meals alone, between meals with others, with lunch, with supper, at dinner with guests, in the evening, to keep awake in the evening or on weekends. Another good example is Lucozade Boost as a drink while recuperating and in need of strength and Lucozade Energy as a sports drink either during or after exercising or sporting activity.

The second approach to user positioning strategy is by associating the brand with a type of user, usually customers or consumers. A good example is Nike with their different kits and wears for specific customer groups; basketball players, footballers, Tennis players, Golf players, swimmers, etc. The problem with user positioning is that if it is too narrow, it will limit the brand's ability to expand its market or user profile.

Celebrity/Person Positioning

This is a situation where the brand is linked or associated with a celebrity or prominent person in the hope that the celebrity will transfer some of those characteristics that he or she is known for to the brand. A good example was Roger Federer when he was a brand ambassador for Nike. Nike even designed a special logo for him, which was used in selling and marketing the line of sports wears designed for and after him. Regardless of the celebrity endorsement for the brand, it is still very important to convince the customers and consumers that your brand is superior to all the other competing brands in terms of design, manufacturing, distribution, etc. Celebrity endorsements for the brand essentially serve as a door opener in the argument and discussion of the brand with the consumers about their chosen brand, especially in the process of trying to convince the customers about the brand's superiority. Celebrities can also be replaced with ordinary men so long as they strike a very prominent cord among the consumers or act as a strong form of emotional connection with the brand or as figurines that represent the desired ethos, image, and expectations of the brand. Inanimate objects like cartoon figures who can be created or modeled along the ideals of the brand can also be used as points of connection or association to the brand.

Lifestyles and Personality Positioning

Every brand either consciously or unconsciously evokes the feelings or perceptions of a personality attached to it. Either due to its style, manner of presentation, or voice/tone of speech patterns, the consumers tends to associate the feelings of a personality to it such that if the brand was a human being; the kind of person it will be; whether the brand will be a warm and vivacious person or a cautious and snobbish person; young, middle-aged or an old person, etc. A decision as to what kind of personality trait a brand should have could be decided on ab initio and then imbued into the brand, or when such personality type is not obvious, it can also be found out through research.

Product Class Positioning

A product class refers to a group of products that are homogeneous or generally considered as substitutes for each other. The product class may be narrow or broad depending on how substitutable the various products within that class are. For instance, as fundamentally different as airlines, trains, and buses are, they all belong to the same product class and are viable alternatives and do compete against one another. This is why for instance, high-speed railways were developed the same as upper-class sections in trains for those who will require luxury and comfort as they travel. In positioning a brand within a product class, you are trying to create an image or identity for the product as well as a reference point whereby the same brand will be compared or measured against. The challenge, therefore, is to still project the brand differences and peculiarities (points of difference) while sharing certain similarities (points of parity) with other products within the product class. For instance, 7UP had to embark on an "Uncola" campaign for its brand, which aimed to emphasize the point that despite the fact that 7UP is a soft drink, it is not a cola-based soft drink, thereby carving out a niche for itself.

Competitor-Based Positioning

According to David Aaker, it is useful to embark on competitor-based positioning due to two reasons; the competitor's well-established image can be used as a bridge to help communicate another image referenced to it. Also, because oftentimes, it may not be important how good consumers think your products are, it might just be enough for them to know or believe that you are better or as good as a well-known competitor.

A formidable example of competitor-based positioning was Texas Armoring Corporation, which produces a range of armored passenger vehicles who, in the course of advertising their product a bulletproof Mercedes car, had their CEO sit in one of the cars with loaded AK-47 magazines being offloaded on the car without any penetration. After such an experiment, it does not take any other form of positioning or advertising claims to dust off any near claims of their competitors.

Competitor positioning is also a prominent means of repositioning competition by changing the prior existing beliefs and thinking within the market about the brand. It is also a good means of carving out a good position for the new brand that has the guts to go against the competition, which most of the time is the market leader. Another good example was Avis, which positioned itself as No. 2 against Hertz: "But we try harder," translated to mean, we make more effort to satisfy our customers because we are aware that we are No. 2.

Country of Origin as a Positioning Strategy
Different countries have different connotations, images, and perceptions attached to them. These countries are also known for certain things such that when you mention them, an image or perception comes to mind. E.g., Germany is known or popular for precision, sturdy, and reliable engineering, Dutch countries for dairy, Italy for leather, France for fashion and delicate or exotic dining and cuisine, etc.

The country of origin of a particular product has a psychological effect and influences consumers' attitudes, perceptions, and purchasing decisions, thereby serving as a cue from which consumers make inferences about the product, and the product attributes. These influences are often based on country stereotypes and experiences with products from that country.

The country of origin usually refers to where a brand is based, a product is designed or manufactured, or other forms of value-creation aligned to a country, and it triggers a global evaluation of quality, performance, or specific product attributes.

According to Cristea Adina et al., a brand's country-of-origin can influence the brand's perceived positioning by reducing perceived risks, acting as a guarantee and enhancer for the positioning strategy. It can influence consumers' buying decision process and offer a significant competitive advantage while it can also, at the other end of the spectrum, negatively affect the brand positioning strategy due to the negative associations with such countries of origin. An example is a connotation previously attached to products made in China or Taiwan.

It is important to note that the country of origin as a positioning strategy must align with the product category's association in order to avoid a negative backlash. Country of origin positioning aligns with the known and existing comparative advantage of nations. You cannot, for instance, launch "vodka" and attach to it a country of origin that is not Russian etc. and expect it to have a positive impact on the market.

At the end of the day, brands, according to Fuchs and Diamantopoulos, are positioned based on tangible brand aspects, e.g., features or on intangible brand aspects like user imagery, which can also be referred to as concrete, attribute-based positioning strategies or abstract positioning strategies. There are also other types of positioning strategies like value positioning, comparative positioning, or endorser positioning (Kalra and Goodstein, 1998).

According to Doyle and Stern (2006), the objective or main aim of the positioning strategy can be to;

- Introduce a new brand into the market

- Change existing brands their positioning or

- Alter beliefs about the brand

- Alter beliefs about competitive brands

- Alter the level of importance or weights given to certain attributes of the product

- Introduce new or neglected attributes

- Find a new market segment for the brand.

Brooke (1994) pointed out some of the reasons why some products are inadequately positioned; either because the segment in which the product is targeted may have become unattractive because it is too small with an inadequate number of customers to sustain a profitable operation, or it has been declining or too competitive or because it has become unprofitable.

The product or brand positioning might also be inadequate because the quality and features that the product offers do not appeal or align with the segment that it is being targeted.

The positioning might also be wrong due to the fact that the product's cost of production, distribution, etc., is too high to be able to allow the product to be appropriately or competitively priced.

Kotler, on the other hand, pointed to four further risks that may cause the product to be inappropriately positioned. They are situations where the product is under-positioned, over-positioned or a situation where the positioning is confused or doubtful.

Under positioning refers to a situation where the full brand essence or potentials of the brand is not capitalized on, projected or expressed, or properly highlighted such that consumers are only vaguely aware of anything special about the brand, its features or benefits or do not even have a clear understanding of the key benefits of your brand. In other words, there is nothing outstanding or special about the brand. It just qualifies as an also-ran product. This is usually a case of the owner's failure to fully characterize the brand or express its full potential as a brand.

Over positioning, on the other hand, is where as a result of too much focus or delineation, the brand is put in a very straight and narrow jacket that does not also fully encompass the full range, profile, and breadth of the brand. Consumers are often filled with misconceptions about what the brand truly represents, often not being able to see or capture its full breadth. For instance, consumers might see the brand as a specialty brand without being aware of the different ranges of everyday brands within its portfolio. It is also a competitive position or product differentiation that may strongly appeal to a few select customers but does not have meaning or significance to a sizeable number of customers enough to reach a firm's sales targets.

Confused positioning, on the other hand, is where the consumers cannot really identify what the brand stands for either as a result of too many and too frequent changes in the brand positioning or where the brand has benefits that contradict each other such that consumers become confused about what the product actually offers. This can also be caused by the brand being associated with too many kinds of things such that it is difficult to clearly pinpoint where or what the brand stands for.

Doubtful positioning, on the other hand, is a situation where the product/brand's claims are divorced from reality or what the consumers' frames of reference are such that they find it difficult to believe such claims. The positioning strategy, in this case, has not been able to effectively convince the potential buyers about the value as well as the benefits accruable from the use of the product.

Brand Positioning Statements
When the outcomes of these analytical processes are crystallized into formal statements, they then become the brand positioning statements. Brand positioning statements are summary statements about the brand's target, market, the category within the same market that the brand is positioned to serve, the major or key differentiator for the brand, or why it is different from all other brands within the same category as well as the brand's payoff or the major statement it is making about itself. In summary, brand positioning statements are comprised of four parts; the target, the category, the differentiator, and the payoff.

These brand-positioning statements, when shared widely across the organization, become the basis of a shared vision for the brand throughout the organization as well as a guide to tactical thinking and implementation across all marketing activities and campaigns for the brand.

Consumers, on the other hand, get to only see or know about these brands positioning as they interface with the brand in its design, pricing, channels of distribution, sponsorships, and other marketing executions as they don't have to see these statements.

A good example of a brand positioning statement is that of Nike, which states that Nike is for athletes in need of high-quality, fashionable athletic wear (target). Nike provides customers with top-performing sports apparel and shoes made of the highest quality materials (category). Nike's products are the most advanced in the athletic apparel industry because of their commitment to innovation and investment in the latest technologies' (differentiator and payoff).

The statement shows clearly that Nike is "for serious athletes, who Nike gives the required confidence to excel by providing the perfect shoe for every sport." It is also positioned as a premium brand. Other customers are lured to patronize the brand based on the brand image, which is enhanced by the distinctive logo and the tagline "Just do it," although they are not the primary positioning target for the brand. The brand is also not positioned as a fashionable accessory, although a lot of people accent their outfits with Nike products.

The external influence promoting the Nike brand is the sports culture of people in the United States and around the world. Sports have become the essence and passion of a lot of people either as a result of trying to be physically fit or being allured by the sports personalities in the guise of being identified with their famous sporting heroes.

Nike regularly partners with sports sensations in the world like Ronaldo from Brazil and released a soccer shoe based on him called "Tiempo Guri FG," which greatly influenced the world's soccer fans. Similar trends were replicated for Roger Federer and Rafael Nadal, where shoe lines with their customized logos were produced. The other external influence promoting Nike is the social status of people. Teenagers, for instance, compete among themselves to become the coolest of all and climb the ladder of social status by wearing Nike sneakers. Such types of brands connect, and their themes are relevant and resonate highly with them.

The Nike 4P's elements based on its positioning distinguish it from its rival competitors. Its products are basically designed for sporting events and are considered to be highly effective and comfortable for athletes. It has dominated the United States sports market. It is recognized for the quality of its shoes and has gained that reputation all over the world. Due to its higher quality shoes, its prices are usually higher than the normal brand. So, the customers perceive it as a high-end product.

The alliance of Nike and Apple brought world sports and music together. Nike and iPod sports kits changed the way people run and created a better running experience. Nike chooses independent distributors and sells its products through about 22,000 retail accounts in the U.S and licensees in other countries. The brand essence of Nike means a unique way of expressing sports in forms of performance, whereas its brand personality is the seriousness of athletes and global representations.

In terms of competition, Nike had no direct competitors because there was no single brand that could compete directly with Nike's range of sports until Rebook came along in the 1980s. Now they have competitors like Adidas, Puma, and Rebook.

Other examples of good brand positioning statements are Coca-Cola and Amazon.

Coca-Cola

For individuals looking for high-quality beverages, Coca-Cola offers a wide range of the most refreshing options—each creating a positive experience for customers when they enjoy a Coca-Cola brand drink. Unlike other beverage options, Coca-Cola products inspire happiness and make a positive difference in customers' lives, and the brand is intensely focused on the needs of consumers and customers.

Amazon

For consumers who want to purchase a wide range of products online with quick delivery, Amazon provides a one-stop online shopping site. Amazon sets itself apart from other online retailers with its customer obsession, passion for innovation, and commitment to operational excellence.

The Connection Between Brand Positioning and Brand Identity

Can a brand positioning exist separate or independent of the brand identity?

Brand positioning, which is the thought, emotions, and feelings triggered in the mind of the consumer when he or she hears and/ or sees, interfaces, or comes into contact with your brand, according to David Aaker, is a part of the brand's identity and value proposition that is to be actively communicated to the target audience, and that demonstrates an advantage over competing brands.

The relationship between brand positioning and brand identity lies in the distinction between intended, actual, and perceived positioning. Intended brand positioning, according to Fuchs and Diamantopoulos, is how a company wants/intends to have the brand perceived by the target consumers. In trying to determine how they want to be perceived, the brand seeks to build an identity for itself.

The fulcrum of the brand's identity lies in the Brand Identity prism that encompasses six major items; the physique, relationship, reflections, personality, culture, and self-image of the brand. This, in totality, is how the brand intends to be perceived. Whether it achieves this objective of how it wants to be perceived by its target audience or not is a different matter.

This intended positioning or perception of the brand lies at the nexus of the interface point between the position with the highest utility for customers, the largest or most profitable customer segment, and the point of being well-differentiated from competitors as well as the associations a company intends to create with a brand.

The actual positioning, according to Fuchs and Diamantopoulos, is reflected in the positioning information actually presented to the consumers (i.e., the execution of the intended positioning and not what consumers finally perceive). This is typically done with different marketing communication tools, advertising, channels of distribution, pricing, sponsorship and events, etc., which are regarded as the main tools for building a brand's position. The question, therefore, is whether there can be a difference between the intended positioning and the actual positioning as exemplified in the actual execution? Examples abound where a wrong interpretation of the correct advertising route or strategy to be embarked upon boomeranged instead of achieving the desired or intended objective. A good example was the introduction of the New Coke formula by Coca-Cola in a bid to ward off competition from Pepsi and other brands.

CHAPTER EIGHT

Brand Analytics and Measurement

The Concept of Measurement

According to the National Council of Teachers of Mathematics (2000), "Measurement is the assignment of a numerical value to an attribute of an object, e.g., the length of a pencil. At more-sophisticated levels, measurement involves assigning a number to a characteristic of a situation, as is done by the consumer price index."

Human beings, in the course of trying to make their lives amenable or understandable to themselves and to one another, come up with several abstract variables, which are constructed to facilitate a sense of meaning, comprehension, and cohesion among themselves. Examples of such constructs are behavior, success, and their various components and ancillaries. With each of these constructs comes the need to measure or quantify them to reflect real-life situations of existence, which ranges from a lack or absence of it to a superabundance supply or presence of such elements.

According to Teacher Vision Staff (2007), for us to be able to assign a numerical value to an attribute of an object, we must first be able to identify the attribute, and then we must have or develop some kind of unit against which to compare that attribute, which often leads to the measurement tools or instrument that supplies us with the units of measurement. These measurement tools are such that they are usually universally accepted or, when uniquely invented, will require a wide level of acceptance before they are accepted as standards of measurement for those attributes. For the measurement tool to be accepted and regarded as precise, it has to possess the ability to measure both the units of the parts of the attributes as well as a coagulation of the units, parts as well as multiples of the whole entity.

Consequently, when you report back to management that your current marketing campaign or effort was successful, what do you really mean? How and based on what parameters do you define or quantify success? If you go further to say that the campaign was impactful, what are you trying to say, and how do you measure impact or what numerical values can you attach to the word impactful, successful, etc. so as not only to make it quantifiable but also to ensure that everyone is on the same page with regards to what you are trying to say and, much more importantly, that your report is objective and not the outcome of a subjective or sentimental evaluation.

Measurement is important because it is one of the basic building blocks to planning. Plans are usually quantifiable and measurable, and not subjective. Embedded in the course of every plan is how those plans will be financed, and at the end of the day, the major or primary source of returns for all the costs spent or incurred in the course of the entire business operations and overhead is marketing and the outcomes or returns from the marketing effort.

Evaluations, on the other hand, are the exercising of judgment or value with regards to the outcome of the measured activity to find out if it does conform to prior established benchmarks or standards of approval.

Why do we need to measure our brands?

Marketing activities are simply actions that are carried out and under the control of marketing professionals, which define or determine the strategic direction of the company. When you take into cognizance the huge investments in brands, results need to be quantified not only as a guide to management decision-making in allocating scarce resources but also as a means of evaluating the entire efforts, energy, time, and other resources invested in the brand. However, research has not only shown the paucity of measuring effectiveness for marketing activities but that also a preponderance of Management executives are not satisfied with the current state of the measurement of marketing activities.

The ability of marketing, despite its agreed importance companywide, to evaluate its own effectiveness will not only lead to greater credibility but also trust within the organization. Not only are marketing departments seen as money guzzlers but also as a group of people grossly lacking in quantifiable measures for their operations.

The measurement parameter for marketing expenditure has always been the outcome of sales but as good as that approach might be, marketing cannot take the credit alone as other departments like sales are also directly accountable for the volume of sales.

One major pushback against measurement parameters in marketing is that measurement is focused on short-term objectives, whereas expenditure on marketing is both focused on short-term and long-term objectives. In managing people and resources, it is an agreed maxim that what gets measured gets done. How can you determine not only the impact of the entire brand activities but also accurately determine the direction and progress of any of the entire brand activities?

Every investment appreciates or depreciates in value over time, so how will you be able to determine the value of your brand over time if there are no accurate measurement parameters for evaluating these brand activities and values over time.

Marketing activities are simply actions, which are carried out and under the control of marketing professionals, which defines or determines the strategic direction of the company.

Each brand is an investment center, with the brand manager acting as the accounting officer for such a brand. Investments in the brand cut across finance, manufacturing, distribution, and logistics, as well as information technology in addition to the actual marketing spend, so an inability to effectively account or measure all these investments to determine their return on investment is a big failure on the part of the brand manager.

According to David Schultz, some of the reasons why marketing measurement has been slow in developing has been as a result of the long time focus on the "four P's," a planning model that relies on managing organizational outputs and not organizational outcomes, as well as the total reliance by marketing and communication on attitudinal measures as opposed to financial measures; an attitude that has led to current marketing behavior toward measurement. The challenge for marketers, therefore, is to either focus on attitudinal, behavioral changes or parameters as the basis of measuring marketing and communication activities or to focus on financial parameters in determining the proper allocation and return of finite corporate resources.

Having said that, however, according to Solcansky and Simberova, the actual measurement or the process of determining the marketing effectiveness is a little bit of art and a little bit of science.

Marketing effectiveness, according to Solcansky and Simberova, is the quality with which managers go on to the market to optimize their spending in order to achieve good results (the objective of marketing; the desired results) within the short-term and long-term period. Short-term results and impacts are measured in terms of profit, whereas the long-term results are focused on the improvement of the brand equity in the minds of company customers, the improvement of the image, market share, etc.

A marketing audit, on the other hand, is the system that checks the effectiveness of marketing activities. According to Kotler, a marketing audit is a kind of independent review of marketing company performance, which aims to identify problem areas and marketing opportunities and to recommend plans aimed at improving the marketing performance of the organization.

The outcome of the marketing audit, if properly implemented, will not only improve the marketing activities of the company but will also improve internal company communications and higher integration and buy-in of marketing staff with the business objectives.

A strategic deployment of marketing audit as an integral activity of the organization other than as an ancillary or ad-hoc activity is one way of ensuring the competitive benefit that can arise from it to the firm. Many forward-looking organizations have been able to achieve this by setting up a market insight and innovation unit as part of the marketing department. This unit serves as the in-house research and marketing intelligence unit.

Marketing measurement, on the other hand, is based on the premise or utilization of certain important metrics of measurement. A metric in itself is defined as the ability to evaluate economic performance using a comprehensive set of indicators that can both be financial or non-financial.

Areas of Marketing Measurement

Brand Equity

The recognition of brands as assets has led to the realization that the return from marketing should not be seen only as the incremental net profit or loss but also as the change in the stored or inherent value of the brand.

Keller (1993) defined brand equity in terms of the marketing effects uniquely attributable to the brand. For example, when certain outcomes result from the marketing of a product or service because of its brand name, that would not occur if the same product or service did not have that name. A good example is Coca-Cola and Pepsi cola which under the condition of a blind taste Pepsi Cola is overwhelmingly preferred, but when the brand name is attached, the reverse becomes the case.

Srinivasan (2005) further broke down the definition of brand equity as the incremental contribution in dollars ($) per year obtained by the brand in comparison to the same product (or service) at the same price with no brand-building efforts.

David A. Aaker, on the other hand, sees the concept as "a set of brand assets and liabilities linked to a brand, its name, and symbol that add to or subtract from the value provided by a product or service to a firm/or to that firm's customers." He grouped these assets and liabilities into five categories, namely: brand loyalty, brand name awareness, perceived brand quality, brand associations, and other proprietary brand assets.

Farquhar regards brand equity as the added value with which a given brand endows a product; a product being something that offers a functional benefit, while a brand is a name, symbol, design, or mark that enhances the value of a product beyond its functional purpose. In other words, the brand bequeaths a life, characteristics, or personae to a product, which is its value or equity. Lassar et al. (1995) included "the enhancement in the perceived value a brand name confers on a product" as the key issue, utility, and desirability in brand equity.

Feldwick summarized and classified the various approaches and meanings of brand equity as the total value of a brand as a separable asset, a measure of the strength of consumers' attachment to a brand, and a description of the associations and beliefs the consumer has about the brand.

Brand equity valuations and measurements, according to Salinas and Ambler (2009), has been one of the critical factors in marketing that has sought to bridge the gap between marketing and finance by justifying marketing investment as well as resource allocation while also acting as a veritable tool of measuring the performance of marketing activities.

The primary capital of many businesses is their brands, and over time, the notion has evolved and come to be accepted widely that a brand has equity that exceeds its conventional asset value. Rank Hovis McDougall in 1988 capitalized its internally created brands, such as Bisto, Hovis and Mr. Kipling, placing a value on them of £678 million, whereas the company's net assets at the time were only around £300 million. This clearly shows that at the time, the value of their brands was worth more than twice the value of the company's assets.

The two main motivations for the studying of brand equity are, therefore, financial in terms of accurately estimating the value of the brand for accounting purposes and to improve the productivity and performance of marketing (Keller, 1993). The greatest value for the brand lies in the knowledge about the brand that has been created in the consumer's mind as a result of all the previous marketing activities and programs carried out by the organization without which no financial valuation will be of any relevance since no value would have been created without that.

Brand equity valuations from the financial perspective have been very useful in the accurate measurement and determination of the company's share prices as well as its assets. They have also been very useful in reporting to the shareholders as to the true nature of their investments and assets, whether as an integral part of the balance sheet or as part of the narrative section of the company's annual report. These financial-based methods of evaluating the brand value are basically quantitative in nature and usually provide monetary values for the brand.

The second sets of parameters for evaluating the brand equity are basically qualitative in nature and are based on consumer behavioral indicators, examples of which are; David A. Aaker's, Kevin Lane Keller's customer-based brand equity, Jean-Noel

Kapferer's, Emnid's brand barometer, Young & Rubicam's Brand Asset Valuator, and McKinsey's method.

Srinivasan et al. (2005), in their own work, came up with a third approach to the measurement of brand equity where the disaggregate individual-level measurement approaches are linked with the aggregate financial-based approach such that the measurements are not only in monetary terms but also allows brand custodians to relate the brand equity to its sources such as brand awareness and attribute perceptions etc.; a marriage of the two major perspectives of measuring brand equity; the monetary/ financial parameters and the measurement based on utilities or customer brand equity measures or parameters.

Brand equity valuations usually come to the fore and take the front burner position in the course of mergers and acquisitions or when brands are being bought or sold. They also play very critical roles in the company's tax computations and other legal issues like break-ups, etc.

Different approaches and methodologies of brand valuation exist in the market today. As a matter of fact, brand valuation has turned out to be a huge market or business with firms like Inter-Brand, FutureBrand, the big four accounting firms all providing their various forms and methodologies of brand valuation, some of which are proprietary methods.

However, according to Keller, all valuations of the brand equity is based on the value created in the minds of the consumers by the marketing activities and programs which he referred to as the "Customer-Based Brand Equity," which he defined as the differential effect of brand knowledge on consumer response to the marketing of the brand.

This customer-based brand equity occurs, therefore, when the customer is both familiar with the brand and holds some favorable, strong, and unique brand associations in his memory with regards to the brand. The basic import of this approach to marketers is that the entire value of their marketing activities is based on the knowledge adding value it has for the customer or not because if it does not have a knowledge (cognitive and affective) benefit for the consumer, then it is a wasted effort. Coupled with that is the real-ization that if these activities do not lead to storage or deposition of knowledge about the brand in the memory of the consumer in the long run, then all the activities would have achieved nothing significantly.

Brand Knowledge
The first point in discussing brand image is brand knowledge. One cannot have an impression, view, or perspective about what he or she does not know anything about. According to Keller (2001), brand knowledge refers to brand awareness (whether and when consumers know the brand) and brand image (what are the asso-ciations that consumers have with the brand).

Brand knowledge refers to a consumer's understanding and recall or ability to remember, say, or associate a brand with the correct brand story, values, partnerships, or its products. The level of brand knowledge can range from being non-existent to being very high.

Consumer brand knowledge, according to Peter and Olson (2001), relates to the cognitive representation of the brand and can be defined in terms of the personal meaning about a brand stored in consumer memory, encompassing all descriptive and evaluative brand-related information (Keller, 2003).

The concept of brand knowledge is an intriguingly and interesting concept because not only does marketing activities create and affect the level of brand knowledge but also that brand knowledge in turn influences both the consumer response to the brand as well as the marketing activities itself (Keller, 2003)

This, however, does not mean that marketing activities are the only source of acquiring brand knowledge open to the consumer. The consumer, by his or her previous knowledge base and experience, must have been exposed to some form of residual knowledge about the brand, its categories, constituents, or their manufacturing processes, which in turn influences or conditions their minds about the brand.

Consequently, an awareness of the brand category, or the needs satisfied by it, the various attributes, features of the brand, the benefits, images, and other visual information about the brand, feelings, and emotions about the brand; attitudes, judgments, and evaluations about the brand as well as previous experience with the brand or its category all join together to form the residue of knowledge available to the consumer about the brand.

Much more than all, these are the indices that motivate a consumer to actively or passively seek knowledge with regards to a particular brand or its category. Human beings are neither tabula rasa nor are they effigies on whom information or knowledge can be forced on. Interestingly also is the fact that knowledge is the outcome of processing information to which the consumer in the first place must have been open and receptive to else no knowledge or information in that particular area will be acquired.

The challenge, therefore, is for the brand to make its information alluring, interesting, and palatable to the consumer before he or she can decide to be open to those information or else no communication (sending and reception of information would have taken place. How to craft or position the information for it to be acceptable to the consumer is, therefore, one of the biggest challenges that the brand will face in trying to make its knowledge acceptable and available to the consumer.

On the whole, two concepts, brand awareness and brand image, combine together to determine the consumer's level of knowledge about the brand. Brand awareness, on the other hand, is made up of two other concepts; brand recognition and brand recall.

Brand awareness, according to Rossiter (1987), refers to the extent to which customers are able to recall or recognize a brand under different conditions; the likeliness that a brand name will come to mind and the ease with which it does so. This sometimes does not necessarily mean that the consumer must be able to recall a specific brand name, but they must be able to recall enough distinguishing features about the brand for purchasing to take place. Brand recall and brand recognition are fundamentally different from each other in the sense that brand recall is associated with memory retrieval, and brand recognition involves object recognition.

Brand recall is also known as or referred to as unaided recall or occasionally spontaneous recall, whereas brand recognition can also be known as aided brand recall. Brand recall refers to the ability of the consumer to correctly generate a brand from memory when prompted by a product category. Interestingly research has proven that most consumers can only recall a relatively small set of brands, typically around 3–5 brand names but certainly not more than seven brand names within a given category.

Brand recognition, on the other hand, refers to the ability of the consumers to confirm that they have seen or heard of a given brand before, which does not actually involve their ability to identify the brand name but just a recognition of the brand on presentation or at the point of sale or after viewing the packaging (Percy et al. 1992).

Top-of-the-mind awareness or the most remembered or recalled brand is the first brand that comes to mind when a customer is asked an unprompted question about a category. The brand that occupies such a position in the mind of the customer is usually considered as a genuine purchase option, so long as the image or the disposition of the brand is favorable. A consumer may, for instance, have a top-of-the-mind awareness for a brand that represents all the negative dispositions of the brand for the customer.

Brand awareness is so critical in the consumer's purchase decision process because purchasing cannot proceed unless a consumer is first aware of a product category and a brand within that category. Consequently, brand awareness increases the likelihood that the brand will form part of the consideration set of brands for purchase. The more aware a consumer is about a brand, the higher the chances that the consumer will be more comfortable with the brand, which raises the chance of selection or purchase of the brand by the consumer. This is so because the greater percentage of resistance to a brand could be cognitive; affection or emotions are usually anchored on some cognitive pillars or hooks.

As a key indicator of the brand's competitiveness in the market as well its performance, several measurement parameters and metrics known as awareness, attitudes, and usage (AAU) metrics have been developed to measure awareness and other dimensions of brand health.

Different Approaches to Measuring Brand Equity: 1. Quantitative Measures

Capital Market Based Approach

Brand valuation using this approach consists of the company's capitalized or realized market value (stock price x number of shares) minus its tangible and its remaining intangible assets (Simon & Sullivan, 1993).

This approach, according to Moisescu (2007), assumes that all factors and events affecting the brand equity (stock price) are immediately identifiable and transparent for all operators of the stock market to be aware of them. However, in actual fact, some of this information, like out-of-stock product, for instance, raw material shortages, etc., may not immediately filter into the stock market or, even when they do, might be very slow in getting the attention of the stock market. Consequently, actual changes or movements in the stock market cannot be attributed to changes in brand value, especially with the prospecting and other activities taking place in the stock market.

The other challenge to this approach is that it can only be used for publicly quoted companies that are listed on the stock exchange and for single-brand corporations. When the company has more than one brand in its portfolio, the pro-rata method of dividing brand equity among a number of brands will at best be only an approximation and not an exact reflection of the actual values of each of those brands.

The Cost Oriented Approach

This approach takes two basic forms; the historic cost-based method, where the brand value is treated as an asset based on the resources that have been invested in it, and the replacement cost-based method, where brand value is treated as an asset-based on what it would cost today to build up an equivalent brand from scratch (Haigh & Perrier, 1997).

The challenge toward these approaches is that the value of the brand does not necessarily increase nor is solely determined by the amount that has been invested into it—the book value. Some of these investments may have been wasted or the subject of several systemic inefficiencies that will definitely not translate to the value of the brand as evaluated by the customers or even the investing public. This approach can also result in the undervaluation of a higher-yielding brand but with lower, more strategic investments.

The other issue also is that both the historical and replacement cost approaches do not take into consideration the future potential, success, or income-yielding capability of the brand as well as the various value-added or lost by the brand as well as the competitive position of the brand in the market.

The License Based Approach
This process of ascertaining the value of a brand, according to Anson et al. (1996), is based on an extrapolation of the license rates obtainable in the industry and earned by comparable brands, which is now translated into monetary terms as a means of determining the value of the brand being assessed. Despite the fact that the license fees are objectively ascertained and obtained from the database of past licensing agreements, it is still doubtful how objectively comparable the reference brands are. For instance, can the licensing agreement fees for Pepsi be a correct replica or representation of the value of the Coca-Cola brand, and could the same be said for McDonald's and KFC?

Licensing fees, in actual fact, are a better reflection of the varying tactics and strategies adopted by the various negotiating parties and not necessarily a reflection of the intrinsic value of the brand.

Price Premium Oriented Approach

According to Crimmins (1992), brand value as expressed in price premiums is measured by comparing the price of a branded product with that of an unbranded one that is identical in all other respects. The unit price differential is multiplied by the quantity sold so as to arrive at the total brand value for the brand.

The drawback to this approach of measuring brand equity/value, however, is that it only takes price and cost data into account while failing to take into consideration different other facets of brand value. Moreover, the underlining assumption of this approach is the presence of a real unbranded equivalent of the branded product, which, if none exists, will give rise to the additional problem of determining a zero or index point as a benchmark.

The other implicit assumption of this approach is that the premium price charged by the brand is a reflection or outcome of the value of the brand. As true as that might be, price is also determined by several other factors, not necessarily the brand value, so assuming that the premium price is just a reflection of the brand value may not be completely true.

At the end of the day, there are different methods and approaches for calculating or determining the value or equity of the brand, some of which are merely academic, technical, or practical in nature. Some of these approaches can be used to restructure the brand portfolio or for managing these portfolios of brands, for budget allocation, as well as for assessing the performance of these brands.

Owing to the fact that marketing activities are in cycles with the output of one cycle acting as an input to the next cycle with the brand equity, according to Ambler (2003), being influenced by the marketer's actions and other key variables in the market and in turn influencing them in return marketing performance can then be measured by short term cash flow incremental as well as an increase in the brand equity represented by changes in the brand's valuation.

These brand's valuations can then be used as a basis of comparing the outcomes of different brand strategies as well as the performance of different marketing teams, thereby improving the accountability and effectiveness of the different marketing activities ranging from defending marketing budgets as well as other marketing decisions like brand extensions or the brand architecture (Ambler & Roberts, 2006).

2. Behavioral Based Qualitative Measures

David A. Aaker's Behavioral Based Approach

Based on his definition of brand equity as "a set of brand assets and liabilities linked to a brand, its name, and symbol that add to or subtract from the value provided by a product or service to a firm/ or to that firm's customers" Aaker distilled and grouped the determinants of brand value as brand loyalty, brand name awareness, perceived brand quality, brand associations, and other proprietary brand assets.

One of the major criticisms of this measurement approach, according to Moisescu (2007), is that the determinants are not mutually independent. Quality, for example, is partly also a function of awareness, associations, and loyalty. Moreover, the factors identified by Aaker are not only determinants but also outcomes of brand equity, so in this respect, they intermix the input and output stages of a brand equity production function.

David Aaker's Brand Equity Model

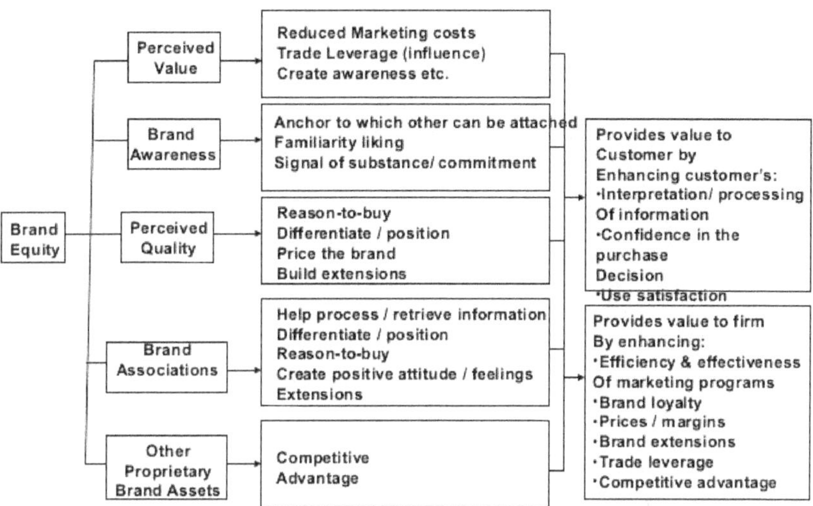

Kevin Lane Keller's Customer-Based Brand Equity Approach
Arising from his definition of brand equity/value as "the differential effect of brand knowledge on consumer response to the marketing of the brand, Keller posited that customer-based brand equity involves consumers' response to an element of the marketing mix for the brand in comparison with their reactions to the same marketing mix element attributed to a fictitiously named or unnamed version of the product or service."

According to Chandon (2003), the different dimensions of brand knowledge can be classified in a pyramid, in which each lower-level element provides the foundations of the higher-level element. In other words, brand attachment stems from rational and emotional brand evaluations, which derive from functional and emotional brand associations, and which necessitate brand awareness.

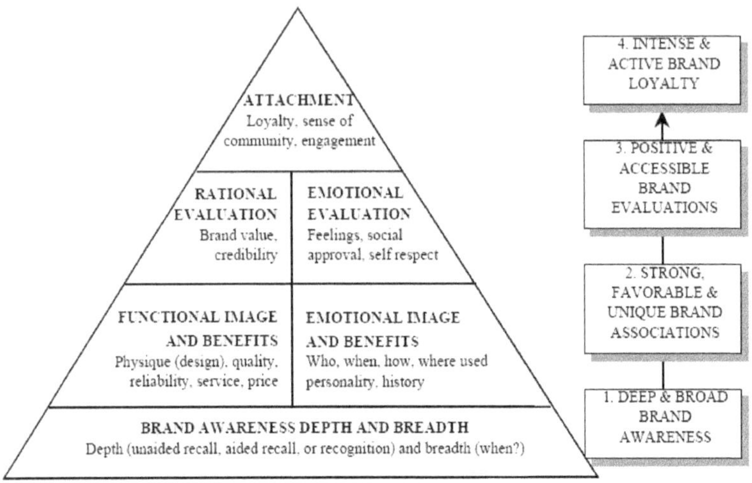

Jean Noel Kapferer Behavioral Based Approach

For him, the brand value lies in a tacit contract between the brand and its customers, who in turn "trade" a seal of quality for automatic repeat purchasing. The utility of the brand name lies in its ability to reduce transaction risk for the producer and consumer alike. The brand's market share, according to Kapferer, correlates positively with brand earnings and is primarily determined by the number of consumers that are loyal to the brand.

Emnid's Brand Barometer

According to Moisescu (2007), this approach assesses brands using a preference barometer on a scale ranging from below average to above average. Criteria used to determine brand preference are unaided brand recall (doubly unaided survey), aided brand recognition (by name only), aided advertising recognition (advertising recently seen), relevant set (aided question about brands in question), trial purchase (trial purchase already made), principal brand (brand currently purchased) and appeal (unaided appeal set).

The major drawback to this approach is that it does not determine the value of the brand in absolute concrete terms, but only relative to the other brands studied.

Young & Rubicam's Brand Asset Valuator
This approach to determining the value of a brand rests on four main pillars: differentiation—which seeks to measure or determine how distinctive the brand is in the marketplace; relevance—whether the brand has personal relevance for the respondent; esteem—whether the brand is held in high regard and considered the best in its class; and knowledge—a measure of understanding as to what a brand stands for.

These four pillars are further broken into fifty-two criteria or components or constructs that are analyzed to determine what the individual components are and what they add up to. Since this is a customized/proprietary method, not much is known about how these criteria are configured or eventually combined to arrive at the final assessment of brand value.

McKinsey's Measurement Approach
McKinsey defines the three P's of the brand as the key determinants of such a power brand: performance, personality, and presence, which they also depose that the quantitative brand strength values are a function of the three P's.

Interbrand's Measurement Approach
For Interbrand, the value of a brand consists of a price that could be obtained by selling the intangible asset evaluated, considering the actual market conditions. The model, according to Moisescu

(2007), uses a scoring system founded on seven groups of factors that bounds a number of eighty specific criteria considered important to the value of the brand: brand leadership (market share, market position, relative market share, market segment, structure, future aspects, etc.), brand stability (history, current position, future development), market (structure of competition, value, volume, trend—market dynamism, prospects), the international reach of the brand (history of international evolution, presence on foreign markets, perspectives), brand trend (development sales volume and market share, competitive trend, development plans), marketing support (advertising activities, sales promotion, future strategy), and legal protection of brand (Rights to name, registration, etc.). The weights of the criteria have been established by Interbrand in an objective way, statistically considering a sample of brands that have been sold along the time. Interbrand relies on longstanding market experience and empirical ex-post studies showing correlations between the prices found to have been realized during company mergers or acquisitions and reconstructions of brand strength.

Brand Image
According to Plumeyer et al., brand image is a major determinant of how consumers feel about a brand and also establishes whether a positive or negative relationship exists between the brand and the consumers. It helps brand/ image managers identify the desirable and undesirable brand associations existing among the consumers and ways of addressing them in their branding efforts.

For Fuchs and Diamantopoulos, brand image is "the concept of a brand that is held by the consumer, a largely subjective and perceptual phenomenon that is formed through consumer interpretation, whether reasoned or emotional."

Brand image is very critical because, according to Fournier (1998), the way consumers perceive brands is a key determinant of long-term business-consumer relationships with the brand. Hence, building strong brand perceptions is a top priority and an issue that cannot be toyed or played with as that is a key determinant of future profitability as well as streams of income.

Aaker (1991), on his own, looked at brand image as a set of associations that are usually organized in a meaningful way and may take the form of anything that can be linked to the memory of a brand, such as product attributes, customer benefits, or relative price.

Keller (1993) considered brand image as consisting of consumers' perceptions about a brand that reflects the brand's meaning and are held in memory in the form of a network of associations. These brand associations may take the form of attributes, benefits, or attitudes.

Brand associations, according to Aaker (1991), are important to marketers and consumers alike because marketers use brand associations to differentiate, position, and extend brands, as well as create positive attitudes and feelings toward brands, whereas consumers use brand associations to help process, organize, and retrieve information in memory and to aid them in making purchase decisions.

It is important to measure brand image and monitor it closely because it has a positive impact on brand trust, customer satisfaction, brand loyalty, brand equity, customers' willingness to pay a price premium, etc., which are all essential elements for building and managing brands.

According to Low and Lamb (2000), despite the importance of brands and consumer perceptions of them, marketing researchers have not used a consistent definition or measurement technique to assess consumer perceptions of brands.

Several researchers and authors have identified and focused on different approaches for measuring the brand image. Research by Plumeyer et al. revealed twelve different brand image measurement techniques such as brand concept maps, constant-sum method, dichotomous scaling, focus group, free-association technique, free-choice technique, in-depth interview, Likert scaling, projective techniques, ranking, repertory grid, and semantic differential scaling.

Some other studies combined Likert scaling with techniques that directly elicit brand associations from consumers, such as the free-association technique, in-depth interviews, and focus groups. Some other studies combined semantic differential scaling with the free-association technique.

Despite these numerous methods of measuring the brand image, Joyce (1963) broadly classified them into two major categories; scaling and sorting. Scaling techniques determine not only whether there is an association between a brand and an attribute but also the strength of that association, whereas sorting techniques merely seek to determine if there is an association.

Likert Scaling

Likert's method of summated ratings (1932), known as Likert scaling, was one of the most frequently applied methods to measure brand image. According to Hair et al., This technique asks respondents to indicate the extent to which they agree or disagree with a series of statements about the stimulus object, that is, the target brand or its associations. Each statement usually has five or seven response categories in a forced-choice format ranging from "strongly disagree" to "strongly agree." After respondents assess their statements, each statement is assigned a numerical score that enables a total summated score or a mean score to be calculated for each respondent, indicating his or her attitude toward the brand.

According to Plumeyer et al. (2017), based on their research, the scale by Martınez et al. (2009) is the most frequently applied scale to measure brand image. This scale considers three dimensions that attempt to assess tangible (i.e., functional image) and intangible (i.e., affective image) attributes and benefits, as well as overall attitudes toward the brand (i.e., reputation).

Aaker's (1997) forty-two-item brand personality scale and Davies et al.'s (2003) forty-nine-item corporate character scale are also some of the other prominently used Likert scale measurements for brand and corporate image. The brand personality scale involves five dimensions of brand personality (sincerity, excitement, competence, sophistication, and ruggedness), while the corporate character scale includes seven dimensions (agreeableness, competence, enterprise, chic, ruthless-ness, machismo, and informality).

The Likert scaling approach to measuring brand image is very easy to understand, construct and administer and provides insight into the strength of already defined or outlined sets of brand associations.

The limitations, according to Hair et al. (2009), are that it offers only limited information on brand image as the scales used in the measurement are limited to cognitive components of brand image. Other dimensions of brand associations like favorability, uniqueness, etc., do not form part of the investigation.

Semantic Differential Scaling

This brand image measurement technique was introduced by Osgood et al. (1957) and uses bipolar adjectives or adverbs as endpoints of asymmetric continuum like bad vs. good, fair and unfair, pleasant and unpleasant, etc. Respondents are then required to rate the target brand on a number of itemized scales, each bounded by one of two bipolar adjectives or phrases. Each response is then quantified by a numerical score, and thus, means responses can be calculated.

Semantic differential scaling, according to Henerson et al. (1987), is most ideal for measuring positive and negative feelings toward a brand or an object. It is also easy to understand, construct and administer. However, the scales need to be thoroughly evaluated and authenticated with a pre-study so as to be sure that it is adequate and covers the important aspects of the brand image to be measured.

Free-Association Technique

This is another frequently applied technique for investigating brand image as well as eliciting brand associations. Respondents receive a stimulus (e.g., a brand name) and are required to spontaneously name or write down everything that comes to mind regarding the stimulus object or name. The primary goal of the free-association technique, according to Deese (1965) and Koll et al. (2010), is to identify or elicit easily accessible verbal associations from consumer memories.

This approach is most ideal in that it allows participants unfettered freedom to express whatever associations that are uppermost in their minds in their own words. It also does not require a trained interviewer to organize and does not also take as much time as other qualitative techniques. The procedures are also easy to understand, construct and administer.

According to Koll et al. (2010), this approach is limited in the sense that it cannot delve into deeper non-verbal or implicit brand knowledge in the process of trying to retrieve verbal and or explicit brand knowledge from memory. Participants, due to time constraints, might also be restricted from retrieving associations that are stored in their memory.

Focus Groups
The focus group approach, according to Calder (1977), is a more or less open-ended, informal discussion about a target (e.g., a brand) among a small group of respondents (eight to ten) in a relaxed atmosphere. The focus group participants are usually homogeneous in demographic and socioeconomic characteristics, hence the need to carefully screen them ahead of time.

There has to be a skilled moderator in the focus group, whose major role is to guide the conversation and ensure that participants focus on the topic of interest. He stimulates the discussion and evokes ideas, opinions, beliefs, feelings, or attitudes from the participant for the duration of the focus group meeting, which could be between forty-five to ninety minutes.

It is also the responsibility of the moderator, with the assistance of the rapporteurs, to summarize the key findings and, if possible, draw a conclusion and issue a report of the outcomes of the focus group study.

The job of recording the discussions and outcomes of the focus group is usually the responsibility of appointed recorders or rapporteurs so as to free the moderator and allow him to pilot the proceedings effectively.

Focus group discussions are good exploratory approaches toward understanding and measuring the brand image as they can uncover how participants conceptualize the brand as well as provide an opportunity for the participants to compare and challenge the experiences of others with respect to the brand as well as provide further background to their positions with regards to the brand (Keller, 2013).

Depending on the skills and professionalism of the moderator, the outcome of the focus group can be biased based on how he directs the discussions or based on the composition of the people and the group dynamics, which can also influence the outcomes. At the end of the day, the generalizability of the outcomes is usually not possible but can be the basis of further studies, etc.

In-Depth Interviews
This approach seeks to elicit in-depth information on brand associations and, according to Hair et al. (2009), usually involves a trained interviewer asking a respondent a set of semi-structured, probing questions, typically in a face-to-face setting.

According to Legard et al. (2003), this approach combines structure with flexibility so as to uncover associations concerning the target brand. The interview is also interactive in nature as it relies on the interaction between the interviewer and the respondent, with the interviewer encouraging the respondent to answer freely.

The interviewer in this approach also uses a range of probing questions to achieve a deeper understanding in terms of penetration, exploration, and explanation. In-depth interviews are also generative in the sense that new knowledge or thoughts can also be created.

This approach offers the flexibility of collecting data on consumers' individual brand associations: attitudes, motivations, opinions, etc., in a highly detailed form, which can also reveal their inner thinking (Hair et al. 2009).

However, due to its highly individualized nature, it makes it difficult to distinguish the various small differences, which does not make for any generalizations. It is also very costly in terms of time, setup, and completion.

The Free-Choice or "Pick Any" Technique
This approach, according to Dolnicar et al. (2012), can technically be described as a free-choice affirmative binary approach. In this approach, the interviewer, according to Barnard and Ehrenberg (1990), presents respondents with an attribute and asks them which, if any, of the listed brands they can associate with that attribute. To avoid order and priming effects, the attributes and the brand list are usually randomized.

According to Swait et al. (1993), the presentation order can be changed by first showing respondents a brand and then asking them which, if any, of the listed attributes can they associate with the brand? The answers are then saved in a binary form.

This approach is most beneficial in the evaluation of similar brands, as participants do not have to select between forced options or choices encompassing unfamiliar brands. More answers are usually received quicker since the brands are all familiar to the respondents. In terms of analytical rigor and options, the reduction of questions to the presence or absence of an association renders the measurement less robust. Results obtained using this approach are usually more unstable and less reliable.

Dichotomous Scaling

This approach, according to Malhotra (2010), is characterized by having only two response categories (such as "yes" vs. "no," "agree" vs. "disagree"), which can be accompanied by a neutral response category reflecting the two categories' inapplicability. To measure brand image, dichotomous questions can reveal whether a predefined association is associated with the target brand and, concomitantly, whether the target brand is characterized by any specific, predefined associations.

This approach is usually apt when the respondents do not have enough knowledge about the brand to make detailed judgments. However, it does not lend itself to analytical rigor, nor does it give any insight into the strength of the brand associations.

Projective Techniques

According to Plumeyer et al. (2017), these are unstructured, indirect forms of questioning that seek to have respondents express their deepest motivations, beliefs, attitudes, or feelings regarding a topic of interest (e.g., the brand). Respondents, according to Boddy (2005), are encouraged to "project" their own unconscious thoughts onto someone or something, and "respond in ways in which they would otherwise not feel able to respond."

According to Helkkula and Pihlstrom (2010), there are four categories of projective techniques;

1.association tasks (e.g., brand personification)

2.completion tasks (e.g., sentence or story completion tasks)

3.construction tasks (e.g., bubble drawings/cartoon tests), and

4.expressive tasks (e.g., role-play).

The strength of this approach, according to Plumeyer et al., lies in its ability to uncover the participants' true opinions, attitudes, and feelings, especially when they are unwilling to expose them. However, it requires highly skilled and experienced researchers to apply as well as interpret their outcomes. They are also very expensive and difficult to administer.

The Repertory Grid Technique
This technique can be used for eliciting personal constructs (i.e., what people think about a given topic) and is based on Kelly's (1955) personal construct theory. According to this theory, people's view of objects that they interact with is made up of a collection of related similarity–difference dimensions. The repertory grid technique utilizes the so-called triads consisting of three stimuli (i.e., brands). In the first step, respondents have to name a dimension in which two of the three brands are similar to each other (i.e., similarity or emergent pole) and, at the same time, different from the third brand (i.e., contrast pole). This procedure is repeated15–20 times to identify important image dimensions. In the second step, respondents evaluate brands on the identified image dimensions using a bipolar rating scale. This allows researchers to assess the relevance of each image dimension and to derive the connection strength between each image dimension and the brands.

The major advantage of this approach, according to Boyle (2005), is that it is able to determine the relationship between brand images as well as identify important image dimensions without researcher bias. It is, however, very time-consuming and expensive to set up.

Brand Concept Maps

This concept is based on the idea that consumers organize information in memory in the form of a network, which in turn led to the introduction of brand concept maps by John et al. (2006) for measuring brand images and underlying brand association networks.

This approach, according to Plumeyer et al. (2017), consists of three stages. The elicitation stage is where researchers identify a set of relevant brand associations either based on existing research or fresh research to elicit such important associations. The subsequent stage is the mapping stage, where respondents use these previously identified brand associations to map their individual brand association networks. In the final aggregation stage, these individually designed brand maps are aggregated based on a set of standardized aggregation rules to obtain the consensus map, which depicts the whole sample's brand image and underlying brand association network.

Brand concept maps are ideal because they identify brand associations, their underlying network of linkages, their strength, their favorability, and their uniqueness (Schnittka et al.2012). However, because a predefined list of brand associations is used in the mapping procedure, participants might overlook individually important brand associations while only concentrating on the listed and mapped brand associations. They are also expensive and time-consuming to organize, coupled with the difficulties involved in generating large sample sizes

The Constant-Sum Method

According to Plumeyer et al. (2017), this approach is used in marketing research for identifying the relative (i.e., comparative) importance of attributes. Respondents are required to allocate a fixed number of points (e.g., 100) among a set of objects (e.g., pre-defined brand associations) to express their relative preference for, or the importance of, each object (Guilford 1954; Aaker et al. 2011). If an association is completely unimportant, respondents assign zero points to it. The more important an association is to respondents, the more points they assign to it (Malhotra 2010).

This approach is unique because, according to Hair et al. (2011), it is able to indicate both the ranking and the magnitude of relative importance assigned to each association. It also enables researchers to distinguish between several brands without requiring too much time (Malhotra 2010).

It is, however, a complex process as participants might face difficulties assigning points to more than a few categories, thereby making them use only a subset of the associations presented in their decision process (Aaker et al. 2011; Iacobucci and Churchill 2010; Malhotra 2010).

Ranking

This is a comparative measure where brands are ranked in relation to competitors according to their association with an attribute. According to Driesener and Romaniuk (2006), for instance, when a brand is ranked first, this means that the corresponding attribute is associated more with that brand than with the other brands.

Ranking is most ideal when several brands are being compared against one another with respect to the performance of the brand association of a brand relative to its competitors. Critical to this process, however, is objectivity, freedom, and lack of any form of manipulation so as to avoid the participants ranking the brands in manners that are incongruent with their own perspectives. Low ranking, according to Driesner and Romaniuk (2006), may be a result of unfamiliarity with the brands rather than a reflection of the poor performance of the association, so adequate precautions must be taken to avoid this in the selection of participants for the exercise.

Each of these measuring approaches can also be further classified based on their features and the things that they emphasize. Some are association-specific, whereas others are output-specific, practical, knowledge-specific, and context-specific in terms of their emphasis and end results.

Association-Specific Measures, according to Plumeyer et al., are so classified based on their ability to uncover brand associations as a starting point for measuring brand image. This elicitation of brand associations can also be direct or indirect. For example, the free association technique, focus groups, and the repertory grid, which elicits brand association directly from respondents? In-depth interviews and projective techniques, on the other hand, indirectly elicit consumers' (unconscious) thoughts and feelings about a brand (Zaltman1997; Supphellen 2000). These detailed insights into perceptions of a particular brand or the full spectrum of brand associations for these brands can be detected. They, however, do not lend themselves to comparability between different brand images, as there are no predefined sets of brand associations that can be used for this comparison.

Likert scale method, the free choice technique, and the constant sum methods can be used for the comparison of brand images between different brands as predefined sets of brand associations are used in these methodologies. Consequently, brands can be measured based on how they rate across these predefined sets of brand associations. The downside for these methods is that they are limited and unable to elicit brand-specific associations. They can only measure how the brands rate on the outlined set of brand associations but not any other association outside that.

Output Specific Features

The outcomes of the various methods differ and consequently form a basis for classifying them based on the types of outcomes that they give rise to. For example, the free-association technique, focus groups, in-depth interviews, and projective techniques provide qualitative (often textual) data, which are usually subjected to further analysis so as to derive the full insight from the identified connection between the brand and different associations (Michel and Rieunier 2012).

Free-choice technique and dichotomous scaling, on the other hand, produce binary data; Likert scaling, semantic differential scaling, repertory grid, and the constant-sum give rise to interval data from which mean values and standard deviations can be calculated (Hagtvedt and Patrick2008; Allman et al. 2016). The ranking technique provides ordinal data, whereas the BCM approach gives rise to network data.

Practical Features

Practical features are based on the appreciation of the cost-benefit ratio of each technique (Plumeyer et al.), arising from the amount of time and effort required to conduct these brand image studies. Techniques such as Likert scaling and the free-association techniques are characterized as easy to conduct and easy to administer, whereas techniques like in-depth interviews and projective techniques require extensive resources in terms of special expertise and time to conduct. Others like focus groups, in-depth interviews, and projective techniques usually require trained interviewers to moderate and achieve the desired objective of prying out the respondents' inner thoughts about the brand. Brand concept maps, on the other hand, are seriously time-consuming to carry out.

Knowledge-Specific Features

This classification is based on the level of knowledge and familiarity with a particular brand that the respondent needs to have before it will be appropriate to use a particular method or technique of brand image measurement technique.

When consumers are not knowledgeable enough to make detailed judgments, dichotomous scaling or the free-choice technique, which is cognitively less demanding, can be used (Hsieh et al.2004). Whereas for highly familiar and knowledgeable respondents, other techniques can be applied to provide deeper insights into brand (image) perceptions (Plumeyer et al.)

Context-Specific Features

Here brand image measurement techniques are classified based on their ability to measure brand image either in a competitive or non-competitive environment. Repertory grid using its triad of brands and ranking, evaluate the image of the brand in the context of other brands, whereas most of the other techniques evaluate brands in a non-competitive environment.

CHAPTER NINE

Case Study—The Nigerian Police Force: A Brand in Need of Re-Branding

Why the focus on the Nigerian Police as a case study for our brand exercise some people might justifiably want to know?

One is that the police is a very pervasive brand, one that is always on your face; one that you cannot avoid but must be in regular contact with as a citizen, whether as a criminal or as an upright citizen.

The police are so integral to our everyday lives that whether you believe it or not, they form a critical part of our day's planning in the route we take to and fro our business or the time we leave or stay back pending the "situation of the road" depending on the type of business you are in. For instance, some people usually embark on their journeys on Sundays when according to them, the road will be free and devoid of so many roadblocks. This is so because a delay at the numerous checking points could be adversarial to the nature of their business or facilitate it.

Nigerian traffic, owing to the nature of our roads, is basically manned by policemen and women due to the absence of street lights, and even when there are street lights, compliance is basically dependent on whether there is a policeman around the traffic light who can jump out or sneak out with their various physical implements to stop or arrest you for beating the traffic light.

As an individual, your safety, as well as that of your property, is largely influenced by the Police. For instance, any accident, unless settled amicably by the different parties, will definitely be settled or referred to the police even after the endless street brawls and "wahala" that must have ensued before such interventions.

So as an institution, the police are a very critical aspect of our everyday living, an institutional brand that we cannot but interface with on a daily basis.

How and Why Are the Police a brand?

Before we step into that, let's ask a couple of questions. Why is it that the British police spend the huge resources they do to maintain, advertise, publicize and even turn the regiment police at the Buckingham Palace into such a circus as well as a huge tourist attraction that it has become? Why is it that the daily routine change of guards at the Buckingham Palace is turned into a huge carnival with the public allowed to watch? Why is it that ordinary tourists are allowed to approach up close to the Buckingham police to even take pictures with them? Why is it that LAPD is a huge money-spinning movie on television every year with different episodes of the crime watch a constant for TV viewers?

Brands are a living memory and reside in the minds and in the subconscious of the people who interact or interface with them. So, either by physically interacting with the British police at the Buckingham Palace or by watching or hearing about their parades and dress, you would have developed a liking or admiration for the police force as well as a positive disposition toward them such that on interaction with them your positive disposition will lend itself to a pleasant or not negative interaction.

By watching LAPD, etc., you would have developed a mental picture of the pervasiveness of the police force such that you would be reluctant or unwilling to engage yourself in any criminal situation. Even when you interact with the police, your mind would have been programmed on how to relate to them or what are the allowable behaviors while interacting with the police. A healthy dose of fear or respect for the police, as well as trust in their efficiency in handling crimes and other such situations, would have been deposited in your mind. Any wonder, therefore, why there is a huge difference between our public perception and reaction to the police in Nigeria and that which is obtainable abroad? Mental programming or branding definitely!

In Nigeria, for instance, despite the mouthing of the slogan—the police are your friends—there is always apprehension about any interaction between the public and the police. It is hardly ever friendly, mainly because of the impression already existing in the mind of the public about the police. For instance, abroad, it is hardly ever conceivable for a motorist to fail to stop when flagged down by the police as the individual is as sure as daylight to end up in trouble and pursued to a rat hole and flushed out, but in Nigeria, people at random speed off when stopped by the police either because they know they won't be pursued because the road-block in itself must have been an illegal one for extortion of money or because they are aware of the lack of resources by the police to pursue after them.

The actual level of success or failure in containing crime is actually resident in the minds of the people. If the people believe that crime does not pay and are aware that no matter how long you run that the long hands of the law will catch up with you, then crime will be an unattractive venture, but if the people believe that might is power and that no matter the crime committed that you can always pay your way out of it then crime will be a much more preponderant occurrence. If people are also made to be a partner in crime prevention such that people are encouraged to report a crime so long as their safety will be guaranteed, then crime prevention and bursting will be an easy thing as most witnesses of crime will very gladly come forward to report or witness to such crimes. However, if there is a backlash from such reporting of crime such that the criminals are not only set free but come back to threaten those who reported them, then fighting crime will be a tall order as every man will mind his own business. At the end of the day, the police is a collective asset that is owned by the people, and the mindset, perception, or views of this institution among the public will determine to a large extent how proficient or effective it will be.

To answer our earlier question, the police force is a brand because, like all other institutional brands, it is not just merely a physical organization or entity but an entity that lives in the mind of the citizens as a collective memory. Every member of the public at one time or the other must have had an interaction with the police, the memory of which lives in his mind and will determine or influence his future interaction with the organization. Even if he has not had a personal experience with the police, which will be rare, he would have heard so many stories or witnessed other people's interaction with the police, which also will influence and determine his perception about the force as well as set the pace for any future interaction with them.

The police force has always communicated the idea, which it will want the public to believe or accept about them, which is that the "police are your friend," and as part of this analysis, let's see how effective that is in line with our understanding of the brand.

As a brand, the brand essence of the police is safety and security, the epitome of it. Such that even if you are being pursued by death and destruction and you run into any police station or office, you will feel secure and protected. How far that is true in our present country is still very much in doubt. Horrific stories of people who sought refuge in Police stations and ended up missing abound that not many people will readily wish to pass a night in the police station as a precautionary safety measure.

However, in its communication thrust, which is usually not very much except when parading suspects, their pay-off line or tag line that "police are your friend" is one of their major communication thrusts. So how would you define a friend? If we are honest, so many issues will immediately come to mind. One is that different people have different pictures or mindsets of who a friend is and who a friend is not. So as a concept, what one considers to be a friend or friendship gestures may not equally be considered likewise by some other people; however, the basic tenets of friendship still remain the same in all circumstances.

Secondly is that the police have a very difficult work or task (if there was ever a more difficult work) to do. People, by their very nature, are sometimes finicky such that what one considers to be respectful might be downright repulsive to the other person. A case in point, a policeman flags you down on the road only to tell you that "your boys are here ooo!" or that "your boys are loyal"; one even went to the extent of saying, "Oga, if anyone is disturbing you, let me know so I can waste them," all in a traffic stop by a policeman. Some definitely will find it exciting that the police on the road are his boys and will definitely "roger" while some other person will ask what in heaven's name does that mean? Flagging me down in the midst of a busy day, regardless of whatever you are going through or grappling with, only to spew out such garbage?

One can even go further to ask, "Is that what they are supposed to be doing?" Do I want a police force that is made up of my "boys," ready to kill or waste people just like that? Some of these thoughts make one cringe, and one cannot help but ask, are there no standard operating procedures, manuals, etiquette, or *modus operandi* for these our policemen? And most especially, how is that in tandem with the brand essence—a professional and efficient police force that the top command will want to project. Does this kind of behavior elicit respect and regard from the masses who are actually the customers to the police force, or do they engender some disdain and lack of respect for the force?

The police everywhere in the world do not like bold, assertive, and knowledgeable individuals; they see them as an affront to their person and their authority. The police also erroneously see themselves as the law as opposed to the enforcers of the law.

To be the law means that they determine what is legal, lawful and what is illegal, whereas to be enforcers of the law, they simply implement what has been codified as the law. However, due to the fact that at the point of interaction or interface with their customers the public, there is no adjudicator as to who has behaved rightly or conducted himself or herself according to the stipulations of the law coupled with the fact that the police personnel has available to him or her the instrument of coercion (his uniform and other accessories like the gun, the taser, the handcuffs, etc.) the instrument of force weighs to his or her own advantage.

The police personnel also have the first access to the procedures of law enforcement and will be listened to first as his or her account is always allowable in law or assumed to be correct since it is believed sometimes erroneously that as an officer of the law that he or she will be on the side of the law—righteousness and will not use the law for personal aggrandizement, intimidation or self-benefit.

The individual citizen, on the other hand, unless there is a video recording or evidence of what transpired, will always be at a disadvantage in trying to stipulate his or her own side of what happened. For instance, if there was no video recording of the policeman kneeling on the neck of George Floyd while he was telling them that he couldn't breathe and eventually passed out, how would there have been evidence to counteract the position of the police personnel.

The policeman or woman is also allowed by law a REASONABLE use of force in the execution of his duties as well as in the protection of himself or herself bearing in mind the nature of their job and the inherent risks involved in the execution of those functions. The onus, therefore, of trying to prove a reasonable use of force, usage of force in self-defense tilts very heavily in favor of the police personnel. So to prove the excessive usage of force against the police personnel is USUALLY a very difficult task.

To be able to prove any misuse of force or deviation from the law, the first point of recourse to the citizen is, interestingly, the police force that the individual wants to complain against the misdeeds of its member or employee. As we all know, there is a force of camaraderie among all professions or organizations where the very first instinct is to protect their own and not to sacrifice their member not to talk of the armed forces where due to the nature of risks to their lives that they face in times of danger and in the performance of their daily duties these bonding among them have grown to be very tight. So when you go to complain against one of their own except the individual is a known deviant or recalcitrant individual, the force will immediately or first of all, try to defend or protect its own even before trying to objectively ascertain the veracity of complaints against their staff.

Due to the nature of their job also, the police are inundated with complaints about their operations and about several different kinds of unimaginable things. They become so used to complaints that if care is not taken, ALL complaints, even the ones that are against them and their own operations, will be treated with levity, especially the complaints against them and their operations.

The police everywhere in the world are hardly ever well-resourced such that you always have a shortage of personnel. Most individuals, due to the negative perception of the police force, will not want to consider a career in policing such that there is an acute shortage of personnel. So for the police force to discipline or bench one of their own despite these shortages of personnel is always a difficult thing. So except in very extreme cases, the police force will always be found to treat with levity the complaint against their personnel.

Another big issue with the police force all across the world, especially in Africa, is the kind of training and psychological exposure that the police personnel are exposed to. A visit to any of the police barracks across the country will definitely be shocking. Except for a few officers' lodges, the police barracks ARE NOT FIT OR SUITABLE for the habitation of any reasonably, mentally well-balanced individuals. This is critical because for any human being to operate maximally, his or her mental wellbeing or state has to be first of all guaranteed. Policemen and women are so essential to the collective wellbeing and existence of all of us that if their own wellbeing is not guaranteed, how can the wellbeing of the individuals that they are employed to safeguard be guaranteed? In some locations, due to the nature of their job, police personnel go on for months on end without seeing or being in the company of their families. Sometimes some of them have been known to sleep at the stations, outside the building, under mango trees, inside their operational vehicles, especially during "special" assignments.

To make matters worse, these same individuals whose well-being and psyche are not well taken care of are further emboldened by the issuance of guns and ammunition. Those who have handled guns do not cease to talk about the emboldening often-invincible effect it has on the psyche of such individuals. When you hand over guns to people that emotionally or psychologically are not at their best to interface with the public, is that not a potential scenario for a catastrophe? Fast forward to a scenario where such personnel with a gun who has been under some very extreme adverse condition is faced with a brash citizen who, instead of massaging the ego of these police personnel, confronts them with the knowledge of their rights. What do you think will likely happen?

Salary and remuneration of the police force to be very honest, has also not been the best. In a situation where the salary of a police officer cannot pay the rent of a habitable building, let alone take care of his family, how in all sense of justice do you expect such a policeman to survive? Of course, most of them will resort to extra-judicial means of making up the source of their livelihood.

In all these situations, essentially, what is available to restrain the conduct of most policemen and women is not any institutional checks and balances but the individuals' self-will, conscience, and self-restraint, which is not good enough. Some societies have come up with body cameras as well as cameras on the police patrol vehicles to record the activities and interface of the police with the public or citizens such that such videos can always be reviewed in cases of controversies or complaints.

As a further check, a separate, objective, and non-partisan unit that is not in any way part of the police hierarchy should be set up to monitor and handle complaints about police activities. These bodies, which can be exposed to police operational training for them to better understand the complexities of the police force but definitely not under the control of the police, will be in a better position to act as an ombudsman between the police and the citizens.

A police complaint officer duly employed by the police cannot handle the complaints, for instance, against his or her superior officer, and even when the officer is junior, a higher-ranking police officer can always be contacted to intervene on behalf of the junior personnel that are the subject of the complaints.

Nigeria Police Operations Viz-a-Viz United Nations International Standards on Law Enforcement

Reading through the International Standards for Law Enforcement, one will get the impression of life in Eldorado, a paradise where everything runs the way it should with unimaginable respect and regards to the individual. Sprinkled all through the document are phrases like, "Every law enforcement agency shall be representative of and responsive and accountable to the community as a whole (xvii)." One cannot but doubt if these are applicable to the Nigerian society or to a society that exists in Pluto.

Police in Nigeria are usually only accountable to their superior officers with no form of accountability to the community at all.

State governors who are the acclaimed chief security officers of the state are only able to give directions and instructions to the commissioners of police in their state: "Provided that before carrying out any such direction the Commissioner may request that the matter should be referred to the President for his directions." Consequently, without the direct instruction of the president, the commissioner of police is under no obligation to carry out the instruction or direction of the governor based on the Nigerian Police Act.

At the end of the day, the philosophical underpinning of the government or of the Police Force is critical to the operational modalities of the law enforcement agencies that we have. If, for instance, there is an acceptance of the fact that "the will of the people is the basis of the authority of government" as stipulated by the UN standards, then you cannot but have a benign government and law enforcement which sees itself as mainly in existence to preserve and protect the interest of the people and not to serve their own interests or the interests of some select powerful and privileged members of the society. Godpower Okereke, in his own paper, buttressed this position. According to him, the *raison d'etre* of any police organization is reflected in the philosophy of policing adopted by the agency and in the content of the legal documents that give police officers their powers.

In such a world, the use of force or the "limitations on the exercise of rights and freedoms shall be only those necessary to secure recognition and respect for the rights of others, and for meeting the just requirements of morality, public order and the general welfare in a democratic society."

According to the UN International standards on law enforcement, law enforcement officials shall respect and protect human dignity and maintain and uphold the human rights of all persons (ix), bearing in mind that human rights derive from the inherent dignity of the human person (v). Law enforcement officials shall at all times respect and obey the law (vi). Law enforcement officials shall at all times fulfill the duty imposed upon them by law, by serving the community and by protecting all persons against illegal acts, consistent with the high degree of responsibility required by their profession (vii). Law enforcement officials shall not commit any act of corruption. They shall rigorously oppose and combat all such acts (viii). Law enforcement officials shall respect and protect human dignity and maintain and uphold the human rights of all persons.

If the law enforcement process is subordinated to the law and the people for whose purpose the law is being enforced other than the people enforcing the law, then there will be sanity in the law enforcement process. The mental reorientation process among the law enforcement group is for the purpose of making them realize that they are not above the law, neither does their job confer any superiority to them above the various individuals for whose benefit the enforcement of the law is being carried out.

This will be a wonderful point of commencement for the rebranding process. The parlance "bloody civilians" are usually freely touted among the law enforcement group as if the civilians who do not belong to the law enforcement cadre are just the scums of the earth.

It is remarkable, for instance, that in police investigations, the interviewing of witnesses, victims and suspects, personal searches, searches of vehicles and premises, and the interception of correspondence and communications; the UN International Standards clearly points out that: "Everyone has the right to security of the person (xxviii), Everyone has the right to a fair trial (xxix), Everyone is to be presumed innocent until proven guilty in a fair trial (xxx), No one shall be subjected to arbitrary interference with his ***privacy, family, home or correspondence*** (xxxi), No one shall be subjected to unlawful attacks on his honor or reputation (xxxii), No pressure, physical or mental, shall be exerted on suspects, witnesses, or victims in attempting to obtain information (xxxiii), Torture and other inhuman or degrading treatment is absolutely prohibited (xxxiv), Victims and witnesses are to be treated with compassion and consideration (xxxv), Confidentiality, and care in the handling of sensitive information are to be exercised at all times (xxxvi), No one shall be compelled to confess or to testify against themselves (xxxvii), Investigatory activities shall be conducted only lawfully and with due cause (xxxviii), Neither arbitrary, nor unduly intrusive investigatory activities shall be permitted (xxxix), Investigations shall be competent, thorough, prompt, and impartial (xl), Investigations shall serve to identify victims; recover evidence; discover witnesses; discover cause, manner, location, and time of crime; identify and apprehend perpetrators (xli), Crime scenes shall be carefully processed, and evidence carefully collected and preserved." One could only wish these standards were enforceable and fully operational; then, it would have been a top-notch police force in operation. However, all across the world, incidences abound where policemen and women are completely intoxicated by the powers that they wield on behalf of society and have turned these powers against the most hapless and helpless members of the society; hence the very urgent need for the rebranding of our police force.

On arrests, for instance: "The Nigerian Police Officer is authorized to arrest any person whom any other person charges with having committed a felony or misdemeanor; (c) any person whom any other person-(i) suspects of having committed a felony or misdemeanor; or (ii) charges with having committed a simple offense, if such other person is willing to accompany the police officer to the police station and to enter into a recognizance to prosecute such charge."

Meanwhile, the UN International Standards on arrests posited: "No one shall be subjected to arbitrary arrest or detention (xliv), No one shall be deprived of his liberty except on such grounds and in accordance with such procedures as are established by law (xlv), Anyone who is arrested shall be informed, at the time of the arrest, of the reasons for his arrest (xlvi), Anyone who is arrested shall be promptly informed of any charges against him (xlvii), Anyone who is arrested shall be brought promptly before a judicial authority (xlviii). Anyone who is arrested shall have the right to appear before a judicial authority for the purpose of having the legality of his arrest or detention reviewed without delay, and shall be released if the detention is found to be unlawful (xlix), Anyone who is arrested has the right to trial within a reasonable time, or to release. Detention pending trial shall be the exception rather than the rule (li), All arrested or detained persons shall have access to a lawyer or other legal representative, and adequate opportunity to communicate with that representative (lii), A record of every arrest must be made, and shall include: the reason for the arrest; the time of the arrest; the time transferred to a place of custody; the time of appearance before a judicial authority; the identity of involved officers; precise information on the place of custody; and details of interrogation (liii), The arrest record shall be communicated to the detainee, or to his legal counsel (iv), The family of the arrested person shall be notified promptly of his arrest and place of detention (lv), No one shall be compelled to confess or to testify against himself (lvi)."

How many times have people literally disappeared as a result of being arrested without any of their relatives having been informed as to their whereabouts or the particular station that effected the arrest, let alone the particular offense for which the individual has been arrested? Some people have even ended up in jail without anybody's knowledge as to what actually transpired, and no effort is made to contact anybody on their behalf.

Perspectives about Rebranding—An Audit

From some people's perspective, a rebranding exercise is purely a cosmetic approach to issues and situations where you adopt a lot of face-saving devices and make-up approaches. If rebranding were to be approached from the cosmetology perspective, it would be looked upon as a facial surgery where you remove and smoothen all the contours and facial bumps that give an uneasy and ugly look to the individual as opposed to papering over the cracks by just applying make-up to cover the facial defects. The problem with the make-up approach is that it does not address the root cause of the problem; it just covers up the lapses momentarily, only for it to show up or appear again later to haunt the individual. A root cause analysis, on the other hand, exposes and makes bare the root causes of the problem such that when the root causes are removed, a brand new facial appearance will occur, which even when further embellished, is guaranteed not to give way or fail with time.

So in rebranding the police force, an effort has to be made to find out what the root causes of these current perspectives or views and opinions in the minds of the public are. How does the public currently perceive the Nigerian Police Force? This is important because the brand as a living memory lives in the minds of its consumers or customers, not necessarily what the brand managers say or the opinions that they hold about their brand but what the customers who daily interface with their brands think about those brands.

In a survey organized by Okereke (1995), the result shows that when asked whether they see the police force as an agent of the federal government or a service agency for the public, 207 (about 98 percent) of the participants answered that the police force is an agent of the government while only five (about 2 percent) of the 212 participants said that the police force is a service agency for the public. This perception as to what their real roles in society are will definitely affect these policemen in the exercise of their duties. It will also affect their perception of the civilian public as well as the degree of force that they will exercise in the carrying out of their duties and also to whom they owe their overall loyalty and allegiance.

Another study conducted by Andreski in 1998 stated that the police are among the worst offenders against the law; they levy illegal tolls on vehicles, especially the so-called mammy-wagon (heavy lorries with benches and roofs), which usually carries many more passengers than they are allowed and transgress a variety of minor regulations. They are allowed to proceed regardless of the infractions of the law if they pay the policeman's private toll.

Okereke, in his own study, also discovered that among the police officers surveyed in their research, more than 82 percent of the respondents stated that police officers should use deadly force (such that can cause death or serious bodily harm) to enforce the law.

The survey also showed that the average level of education of the police officers surveyed in terms of years was just 9.3 years, meaning that most of them were not more than junior secondary school graduates having not even finished secondary school.

Most of them were of the opinion that remuneration (salaries and promotion) and welfare of the officers was very poor, equipment insufficient as well as the number of personnel. One of the police respondents to the survey had this to say: "I would like to add that police treatment by the government is so poor that they do not consider us as human beings who take risks day in day out because of our fellow human beings. Police are always exposed to danger pursuing armed robbers day in day out. Yet no prompt promotion, salary very small, no allowances, no accommodation like other forces. In short, we are not regarded as civilians or armed forces."

Orole, Gaddar, and Hunter (2015) pointed out in their own study that the Nigerian public has consistently perceived its police force as one of the least effective in the world, due largely to the endemic corruption that pervades the policing architecture.

This position is more exacerbated by further comments by different people surveyed in the course of their research, especially that of Mohammed Abubakar, Nigeria's former inspector general of police, when he assumed the leadership of the police force on February 13, 2012. "The Nigeria Police Force has fallen to its lowest level and has indeed become a subject of ridicule within the law enforcement community and among members of the enlarged public. Police duties have become commercialized. Our men are deployed to rich individuals and corporate entities such that we lack the manpower to provide security for the common man."

Our investigations departments cannot equitably handle matters unless those involved have money to part with. Complainants suddenly become suspects at different investigation levels following spurious petitions filed with the connivance of police officers. Our police stations, State CID, and operations offices have become business centers and collection points for rendering returns from all kinds of squads and teams set up for the benefit of superior officers. Our Special Anti-Robbery Squads (SARS) have become killer teams, engaging in deals for land speculators and debt collection. Toll stations in the name of check-points adorn our highways with policemen shamelessly collecting money from motorists in the full glare of the public."

To cap it off, Joseph Campbell of the Council of Foreign Relations pointed out that the Nigerian police are chronically underfunded and under-trained, and the police are too often unequipped to deal with local security issues, thereby forcing the Nigerian military to step in and establish order. The army is now deployed in thirty of the thirty-six states, mostly doing police work and undercutting the credibility of the NPF. Also, according to him, police salaries are low. Recruits make less than $400 a year before the last salary increase (though they also receive allowances), forcing many police officers to engage in corrupt practices just to scrape by.

In 2017, for instance, the World Internal Security and Police Index (WISPI) released by two bodies, the International Police Science Association (IPSA) and the Institute for Economics and Peace (IEP), rated Nigeria's police force at the 127th position in the global ratings of police forces across the world, out of 127 countries that were ranked. Botswana was 47th in the world and the best in Africa. Uganda, Kenya, the Democratic Republic of Congo (DRC), and Nigeria made it an African quartet at the bottom—occupying slots 124 to 127, respectively.

According to a survey conducted by Afro Barometer across eighteen African countries, the police are, on average, perceived to be the most corrupt among eight key government and societal institutions. Almost half (48 percent) of respondents say "most" or "all" of the police in their country are corrupt, far outstripping the proportion who perceive widespread corruption among members of parliament (38 percent), tax officials (35 percent), judges and magistrates (35 percent), and presidency officials (35 percent). Fewer than half (45 percent) say they trust the police "somewhat" or "a lot," making them less trusted than presidents and their staff (50 percent), traditional leaders (57 percent), and religious leaders (68 percent).

In eleven of eighteen countries, the police are ranked as the most corrupt institution. In several countries, such as Gabon, Mali, and Guinea, perceived corruption is high across many government institutions. But in others, most notably Kenya, Uganda, Sierra Leone, Nigeria, Côte d'Ivoire, and Ghana, the police stand out as being far more corrupt than other government institutions, by margins of 15 to 24 percentage points.

Interestingly, according to the report, perceptions that the police are corrupt are higher among citizens with more education (67 percent to 69 percent among those with at least a secondary education, vs. 44 percent among those with no formal education). Africans who experience at least some degree of poverty or deprivation are also significantly more likely to see the police as corrupt (61 percent to 64 percent) compared to those with no experience of poverty (48 percent).

The survey also showed that in relation to trust for the police force, Nigerians, Gabonese, and Sierra Leoneans are least trusting of their police; only one in four say they trust the police "somewhat" or "a lot." In comparison to other state institutions (i.e., the presidency, parliament, local government, courts, and revenue authorities), the police are the least trusted institution in Nigeria, Sierra Leone, Ghana, and Kenya, but they are the most trusted in Namibia, Botswana, and Burkina Faso.

What Is Rebranding?

Rebranding, according to the Economic Times of India, is the process of changing the corporate image of an organization as well as its market strategy, of giving a new name, symbol, or change in design for an already-established brand. The idea behind rebranding, therefore, is to create a different and sustainable identity for a brand, from its competitors, in the market.

It will therefore be relevant to find out what are those elements that make up the image of an organization and how does an organization end up with the image that it currently has that may require changing.

Suppose we pursue further our earlier thesis on cosmetology as a basis of illustration. The rebranding exercise, which is applicable to an already existing brand, can be likened to the four basic processes of make-up. The first process is to determine which particular type or tone/color of make-up is most ideal or suitable to the particular skin color in question. All make-up colors, no matter how expensive or delicately made, are not suitable for all skin tones or colors. This process of trying to find out the particular shade or color of the make-up that is best suitable and expresses best the facial features can be likened to the brand identity creation process, the research, and all other processes that go into them. Every skin is unique in its own way, the same as a brand. If a brand loses its uniqueness, then it falls into the category of a commodity.

The next stage after the skin tone and correct match of make-up has been determined is to thoroughly wash the face before applying any make-up. This is aimed at removing all the facial oils and dirt that can negatively interface with the make-up color and mar it or make it not give the expected output. In the same way, brands in their current form and existence could be surrounded by a lot of negative feelings and perceptions that need to be radically addressed or removed for the brand to possess a chance of thriving again in the marketplace. This procedure can be likened to the three processes of segmentation, differentiation, and positioning. This is so because even if you create a unique brand identity and it is targeted to the wrong market segment, it will still fail or if the brand is not effectively differentiated from the existing clutter in the market or if the positioning is wrong and not distanced from all the negative perceptions in the market the brand will still fail.

This is also bearing in mind there is currently a possibly negative perception in the minds of the public that needs to be addressed by presenting some new sets of evidence that can make the public change their negative perception about the brand, which is actually the real essence of the rebranding effort.

After the face has been thoroughly washed and scrubbed of all previous layers of make-up, dirt, and negative portrayals, the new make-up color, etc., will now be applied. In brand management, this can be likened to the process of brand communication, acti-vation, sponsorships, events, etc., that aims to bring the brand to life and ensure a fruitful interaction with the relevant public. The essence of this is to project the new image of the brand so as to create some sets of positive perceptions and associations around the brand in its new form.

Finally, after applying the make-up, the prospects seek feedback on the effectiveness of all the activities that have been carried out either by looking at the mirror or by asking people—how do I look? The brand also actively seeks feedback either from its performance in the market, its bottom-line or other forms of feedback to evaluate all the activities that have been carried out by the brand. These feedbacks are now fed back to the brand identity creation team as well as the communication and activation teams either as a validation of what has been done or areas that need to be corrected or tweaked.

Rebranding, therefore, is basically an exercise aimed at reconnecting the organization with its customers. It can be proactive when due to the dynamic and changing business landscape, the organization realizes that there are opportunities for growth and innovation or that they need to tap into new businesses or customers, which its current image or profile is not conducive or appropriate to maximize such opportunities hence the need for rebranding.

Rebranding can also be reactive when a certain situation in its current environment of operation makes it impossible for its continued existence as a brand or in the same shape or form that it existed before. Such situations can be a result of fraud, as was the case with Enron Energy and Andersen Consulting when they were indicted in the Enron saga. Mergers and acquisitions, new ownership, or as a result of litigation or negative perception by the public, which are all credible grounds for rebranding the organization.

Katharine Paljug (2018), on the other hand, is of the view that rebranding is necessary to encourage growth and clarify the services of the organization. Rebranding is also a means of ensuring that all the negative associations with a brand that has a bad reputation are dispelled or ameliorated. Rebranding is also a means of refreshing or updating an old, outdated, or old-fashioned brand so as to make it more contemporary and acceptable within its customer base. A good example is the Rebranding exercise of First Bank in 2004 that led to all the massive rebranding exercises in most of the banks in Nigeria, which yours truly was a major player in the process.

One of the unique aspects of service organizations is that their services are often embedded within their existence. Using the police force as an example, you cannot differentiate or create a partitioning between the force and its various services like the arrest of criminals or suspects, investigation of crimes, safeguarding of lives and properties, etc. In as much as the force can create administrative units to carry out each of these activities, all of them congregate to create a single image or perception about the service.

In rebranding an organization like the police force, therefore, the essential ingredients to focus upon are the personnel, the services rendered as well as the environment in which the services are rendered. The corporate outlook of the organization can only do good in the sense of trying to reorient the minds of the public or point out to them the rebranding exercise that has taken place.

In looking at each of these elements, the personnel are very important to the image of the organization. This is important because the image of the organization that the public will ever have are the image or impressions acquired by them on contact with the employees of the organization, in this case, the police officers. If they are courteous, respectful, knowledgeable and disciplined, etc., not easily infuriated, the public in contact with them will definitely develop a very good impression about the organization. But if, on the other hand, the employees are people who tout AK-47s about with a threat to shoot at the slightest provocation or contact—people who are not amenable to reason but are only interested in extorting money from people under different kinds of threat—then the impression the people will develop about them can be imagined.

A major chip in this suggested rebranding exercise for the police force hinges on the men and officers of the force. If they can be oriented to see the citizens as human beings who they have been recruited to serve and not lord over, then a huge milestone would have been achieved in the rebranding and repositioning of the police force.

The second aspect of the rebranding exercise is the services rendered by the policemen and women. Services are unique in that they cannot be stored; they are consumed as they are being created. The other thing unique about service is that their quality is in direct proportion to the skills and competence of the person providing the service. One person rendering the same service might be courteous and smiling, while another person rendering the same service as in the case of receptionists can be hostile and cantankerous.

The onus, therefore, rests on the organization to upscale the skills and competencies of their employees while ensuring that they have the right attitude for their job. The organization should also stipulate and set standards and operating manuals as a guide to the employees to ensure that the quality of their service at all-time equates to the standards set. Without set standards that also need to be strictly monitored and deviations disciplined, there will be no way to ensure compliance or consistency in the quality of services rendered.

The environment in which the services are rendered is the other important element in the rebranding/branding of services. The ambiance of the environment in which the services are rendered is so key that it is vital for the psyche of both the people rendering the services as well as the people to whom the services are being rendered. Maybe key in this whole equation might be the failure of the force to appreciate and understand that policing is actually a service being rendered to the public, and it is so vital and important how that service, as well as any other services, is rendered. Policing has the capacity of infringing and limiting the freedom and liberties of the individual.

If this factor is appreciated, then there should be a major and massive remodeling resurfacing of almost all the police stations in this country. The waiting rooms, interrogation rooms, etc., are so austere, hostile, unfriendly, and uninviting. No person who really does not have a vital reason to be there can afford to be there for a reasonable amount of time.

Finally, the corporate logo, colors, and corporate function materials for the police force, in my own estimation, is a beautiful rendition that immediately strikes a clear brand awareness or recognition among the public. It also inspires respect. As a matter of fact, the only thing that is abysmal about it is the unwillingness of men and officers of the force to appear in the correct uniform and attire of the force. Some will wear all manner of shoes, loafers, and even slippers alongside their uniforms; others will put on all manner of clothes, T-shirts, polos, and different kinds of tops without conforming to the police regulatory uniforms. Efforts should therefore be focused on enforcing compliance among the officers and men of the force in adopting the correct uniforms and appearance of the force.

The operational vehicles are also another very sore sight and low point for the force. The vehicles are hardly ever in good shape, with a lot of them dilapidated or dented. In some instances, you can also see the members of the force huddled in all manner of unbranded vehicles such that if care is not taken, one might wonder if they are men of the underworld.

A rebranding effort will therefore require a huge reorientation that will enable the men and officers of the Nigerian police force to place the broad interests of the general public first in all decisions affecting its operations in line with their existing vision statement, which is "to make Nigeria safer and more secure for economic development and growth; to create a safe and secure environment for everyone living in Nigeria."

The values of the Nigerian police force are also germaine, as well as the provision included in it "to continuously evaluate and improve police services." It will be important to carry out an independent and unbiased analysis, survey, or review of the police force on a regular basis to find out how they have lived up to their core values of working together with people irrespective of religious, political, social, or economic affiliations to:

- Deliver quality police service that is accessible to the generality of the people.

- Build a lasting trust in the police by members of the public.

- Protect and uphold the rights of persons; to be impartial and respectful in the performance of police duties.

Why is such an exercise necessary at such a time like this?

At the center of the current political rumblings and protests across the country is an agitation against the police force and its operational modalities. For the masses of a nation to rise in protest against one of its fundamental agencies of governance like the police is quite fundamental and should not be pushed aside.

The rebranding exercise will give the police force a very good opportunity to holistically address all the issues raised by the different parties, and in doing that, they will be assured of support from all the strata of the society.

Trust is an enduring ingredient required for any agency or parastatal of government to operate, and if this trust is lost, then some fundamental issues are at stake. The police force is so strategic and vital to the effective functioning of any society, such that its efficiency cannot be toyed with.

Organizations and parastatals, from time to time, reinvent themselves or reorganize and refashion their operations so as to ensure that they still remain and maintain their relevance to their relevant public. So this might be a good opportunity for the Nigerian police force to reinvent itself and ensure its continued relevance to the Nigerian public.

Reference

Chuck Densinger and Mason Thelen (2015) The Brand Triangle. Online Resources. Retrieved From: https://elicitinsights.com/blog/the-brand-triangle-part-2/

Susan Gunelius (n.d) Brands or Products What is the Difference? Online Resources. Retrieved From: https://aytm.com/blog/brand-product-difference/

ActivistBrands.com (n.d) What is Brand Activism. Online Resources. Retrieved From: http://www.activistbrands.com/what-is-brand-activism/

Gilman Steve (2017) What is Brand Architecture. Online Resources. Retrieved From: https://www.gravitygroup.com/blog/what-is-brand-architecture/

Dennise Lee Yohn (2017) 9 different Types of Brands. Online Resources. Retrieved From: https://deniseleeyohn.com/9-different-types-of-brands/

Derek Smith (2020) Why brand Architecture Matters and What to Do About It. Online Resources. Retrieved From: https://elementthree.com/blog/why-brand-architecture-matters-and-what-you-can-do-about-it/

Designate (n.d) Why Investor Brand matters and how to make it work for you. Online Resources. Retrieved From: https://www.designate.com.au/insights/why-investor-brand-matters

Kali Halk (2017) What is Product Branding and why it is essential in retail. Online Resources. Retrieved From: https://www.shopify.com.ng/retail/what-is-product-branding-and-why-its-essential-in-retail

Mark Di Somma (2015) 21 Different Types of Brand. Online Resources. Retrieved From: https://www.brandingstrategyinsider.com/18-different-types-of-brand/#.X5sUTh0o_8M

Filipa Amado (2019) Elements of Value. Online Resources. Retrieved From: https://snowball.digital/blog/the-elements-of-value

Marshal (n.d) Brand Architecture Examples. Online Resources. Retrieved From: https://www.marshallstrategy.com/our-services/brand-architecture/brand-architecture-examples/

Sarah Lybrand (2018) What is Employer Branding and How it can grow your business. Online Resources. Retrieved From: https://business.linkedin.com/talent-solutions/blog/employer-brand/2018/employer-branding

PersonalBrand.com (n.d) Official Definition of Personal Brand. Online Resources. Retrieved From: https://personalbrand.com/definition/

The Challenger Project (n.d) Online Resources. What is a Challenger Brand? Retrieved From: https://thechallengerproject.com/blog/what-is-a-challenger-brand

Leslie de Chernatony and Susan Segal-Horn (2000) The Criteria For Successful Service Brands. Online Resource. Retrieved From: https://pdfs.semanticscholar.org/c44b/a38cffe8dbb803834fd9b82d37f631a39c9b.pdf

Michael Stelzner (2019) Personal Branding: How to successfully Build your Brand. Online Resources. Retrieved From: https://www.socialmediaexaminer.com/personal-branding-how-to-successfully-build-brand-rory-vaden/

Corinne Rochette (2015) The public brand between new practices and public values. International Review of Administrative Sciences https://doi.org/10.1177/0020852315579328

Placebrandobserver.com (2019) Public Vs. Private Sector Branding Explained: Similarities and Differences. Online Resources. Retrieved From: https://placebrandobserver.com/public-private-sector-branding-similarities-differences/

Pauline Kerr (2013) Diplomacy in a globalizing world: theories and practices

Hinge University (2018) Differentiation Guide For Professional Services Firms. Online Resources. Downloaded From: https://hingemarketing.com/wp-content/uploads/2018/10/Guide-Differentiation-2nd-1.pdf

Hwajung Kim (2012) The Importance of Nation Brands. Online Resources. Retrieved From: http://www.culturaldiplomacy.org/pdf/case-studies/Hwajung_Kim_The_Importance_of_Nation_Brand.pdf Alice Tybout and Tim Calkins (2005) ed Kellogg on Branding. Wiley

John Tyreman (2019) Developing Differentiators: How Research can help you pass the test. Online Resources downloaded From: https://hingemarketing.com/blog/story/developing-differentiators-how-research-can-help-you-pass-the-test

Elizabeth Harr (2020) Competitive Differentiation: A Playbook for winning in a congested marketplace. Online Resources Downloaded From: https://hingemarketing.com/blog/story/competitive-differentiation-a-playbook-for-winning-in-a-congested-marketplace

Career Guide (2020) Differentiation Strategy: Definition, Benefits and Creation. Online Resources. Retrieved From: https://www.indeed.com/career-advice/career-development/differentiation-strategy

Casey Newman (2018). What is a Value Proposition? (Plus 3 Great Examples and 3 Common Mistakes. Online Resources. Retrieved From: https://www.kunocreative.com/blog/good-value-proposition-examples.

Josh Porter (n.d). How to Communicate Product Value. Online Resources. Retrieved From: https://mixergy.com/course-cheat-sheet-communicating-product-value/

Lorraine Carter (2014) Brand Differentiation: 30 Ways to Differentiate Your Brand. Online Resources. Retrieved From: https://www.personadesign.ie/brand-differentiation-30-ways-to-differentiate-your-brand/

Aaron Brooks (2020) 30 Killer Examples of Personalized Customer Experiences. Online Resources. Retrieved From. https://www.ventureharbour.com/personalised-experiences-examples/

Zoovu (2017), How 3 Brands Establish Themselves as Experts to Rise Above the Competition. Online Resources. Retrieved From: https://zoovu.com/blog/3-brands-establish-themselves-as-experts/

Eric Almquist, John Senior and Nicolas Bloch (2016), The Elements of Value Measuring—and delivering—what consumers really want. Online Resources. Retrieved From: https://hbr.org/2016/09/the-elements-of-value

Africa Facts (n.d) Online Resources. Retrieved From: https://africa-facts.org/botswana-police-ranked-africas-best-nigeria-at-bottom-of-global-report/

Josephine Appiah-Nyamekye Sanny and Carolyn Logan (2020) Citizens'negative perceptions of police extend well beyond Nigeria's #EndSARS Online Resources. Retrieved From: https://afrobarometer.org/sites/default/files/publications/Dispatches/ad403-negative_perceptions_of_police_go_well_beyond_nigeria-afrobarometer_dispatch-v4-5nov20.pdf

Okereke, G. O. (1995). Police officers' perceptions of the Nigeria Police Force: Its effects on the social organization of policing. Journal of Criminal Justice, 23(3), 277–285. doi:10.1016/0047-2352(95)00014-h

Orole, F. A, Gadar, K. B. and Hunter, M (2015) INFLUENCING FACTORS AND THEORETICAL PERSPECTIVE OF POLICE CORRUPTION IN NIGERIA. International Journal of Social Science & Human Behavior Study–IJSSHBS Volume 2: Issue 2 [ISSN: 2374-1627]

Joseph Campbell (2018) Nigerian Police are in Desperate Need of Reform. Online Resources. Retrieved From: https://www.cfr.org/blog/nigerian-police-are-desperate-need-reform.

Economic Times of India (2021) Rebranding. Online Resources Downloaded From: https://economictimes.indiatimes.com/definition/rebranding

Katharine Paljug (2018) Rebrand Your Business without Losing your Audience. Online Resources. Retrieved From: https://www.businessnewsdaily.com/8764-business-rebranding-tips.html

TeacherVision Staff (2007) The Concept of Measurement. Online Resources. Retrieved From: https://www.teachervision.com/measurement/the-concept-of-measurement

Solcansky, M and Simberova, I (2010) MEASUREMENT OF MARKET-
ING EFFECTIVENESS. ECONOMICS AND MANAGEMENT. Online
Resources. Retrieved From: https://www.researchgate.net/profile/
Marek-Solcansky/publication/266489513_MEASUREMENT_OF_
MARKETING_EFFECTIVENESS/links/545bdd710cf2f1dbcbcb0676/
MEASUREMENT-OF-MARKETING-EFFECTIVENESS.pdf

Plumeyer, A, Kottemann, P; Böger, D, and Decker, R (2017), Measuring
brand image: a systematic review, practical guidance, and future research
directions. DOI 10.1007/s11846-017-0251-2
Fournier (1998)

George S. Low Charles W. Lamb Jr, (2000), "The measurement and
dimensionality of brand associations," Journal of Product &Brand
Management, Vol. 9 Iss 6 pp. 350—370

Salinas, G, and Ambler, T (2009) Journal of Brand Management (2009)
17, 39—61. DOI: 10.1057/bm.2009.14

Aaker DA, Kumar V, Day GS, Leone RP (2011) Marketing research.
Wiley, Hoboken

Ambler, T . (2003) Marketing and the Bottom Line, 2nd ed. London: FT
Prentice-Hall.

Ambler, T . and Roberts, J . (2006) Beware the Silver Metric: Marketing
Performance Measurement has to be Multidimensional. Marketing
Science Institute, Report No. 06 113, October.

Barnard NR, Ehrenberg ASC (1990) Robust measures of consumer brand
beliefs. J Mark Res27(4):477–487

Boddy C (2005) Projective techniques in market research: valueless
subjectivity or insightful reality? A look at the evidence for the usefulness,
reliability and validity of projective techniques in market research. Int J
Mark Res 47(3):239–254

Boyle TA (2005) Improving team performance using repertory grids. Team Perform Manag Int J 11(5/6):179–187

Chandon, P (2003) Faculty & Research Note on Measuring Brand Awareness, Brand Image, Brand Equity and Brand Value. Online Resources. Retrieved From: http://courseware.cutm.ac.in/wp-content/uploads/2020/06/2003-19.pdf

Davies G, Chun R, Da Silva R, Roper S (2003) Corporate reputation and competitiveness. Routledge, London

*Dolnicar S, Gruen B (2014) Including don't know answer options in brand image surveys improves data quality. Int J Mark Res 56(1):35–49

Dolnicar S, Rossiter JR (2008) The low stability of brand-attribute associations is partly due to market research methodology. Int J Res Mark 25:104–108

*Dolnicar S, Rossiter JR, Grun B (2012) "Pick-any" measures contaminate brand image studies. Int JMark Res 54(6):821–833

*Driesener C, Romaniuk J (2006) Comparing methods of brand image measurement. Int J Mark Res48(6):681–697

Hair JF, Bush RP, Ortinau DJ (2009) Marketing research. In a digital information environment, 4th ed. McGraw-Hill Irwin, Boston

Hair JF, Celsi MW, Money AH, Samouel P (2011) Essentials of business research methods. Sharpe, Armonk

*Hsieh MH (2002) Identifying brand image dimensionality and measuring the degree of brand globalization: a cross-national study. J Int Mark 10(2):46–66

*Hsieh MH, Lindridge A (2005) Universal appeals with local specifications. J Prod Brand Manag14(1):14–27
Joyce T (1963) Techniques of brand image measurement. New developments in research. Market Research Society, London

Keller KL (2003) Strategic brand management: building, measuring and managing brand equity. Prentice-Hall, Upper Saddle River

Keller KL (2013) Strategic brand management: building, measuring, and managing brand equity. Pearson, Harlow
Keller KL (2016) Reflections on customer-based brand equity: perspectives, progress, and priorities.AMS Rev 6(1):1–16

Likert R (1932) A technique for the measurement of attitudes. Arch Psychol 22(140):5–55

Low GS, Lichtenstein DR (1993) Technical research note: the effect of double deals on consumer attitudes. J Retail 69(4):453–465

Malhotra NK (2010) Marketing research: an applied orientation. Prentice-Hall, Upper Saddle River

Romaniuk J (2013) Modeling mental market share. J Bus Res 66(2):188–195

*Romaniuk J, Sharp B (2000) Using known patterns in image data to determine brand positioning. Int JMark Res 42(2):219–229

*Romaniuk J, Bogomolova S, Dall'Olmo Riley F (2012) Brand image and brand usage: Is a forty-year-old empirical generalization still useful? J Advert Res 52(2):243–250

Rossiter, J.R. (1987). Advertising and Promotion Management. New York: McGraw-Hill Series in Marketing.

Kevin Lane Keller (2003) Brand Synthesis: The Multidimensionality of Brand Knowledge. Journal of Consumer Research, Vol. 29, No. 4, pp. 595-600

Peter, J. Paul and Jerry C. Olson (2001), Consumer Behavior, Chicago: Irwin.

About the Book

This book, in its journey, started with an attempt to understand and clarify the meaning and origin of the word "brands," the basic differences between a brand and a product or service. From there, it looked at the different types of brands as well as the architecture of these brands or how they have been organized over the years. From there, the book then took a leap into an exploratory study of several brands and the various factors responsible for their successes and failures.

Several organizations, as well as industry practitioners, have spent several hours as well as huge amounts of money to find the answer to the critical factors responsible for the successes as well as the failures of brands. This book is merely an attempt to approach the complex field of brand management in a manner that seeks to demystify and clarify the concept of brands and what any brand practitioner should know about the key indices responsible for the success and failures of their brands.

• • •

Reference is made all across the book to the major insights and thoughts of prominent authors and trailblazers in the field of brand management, just like the famous saying, *"If I am standing tall today, it is merely because I stand on the shoulders of several others who have gone before me."*

About the Author

Emmanuel Obeta is an accomplished and results-oriented executive with over thirty years of extensive experience leading corporate marketing, communications, brand management, leadership and strategic operations for multimillion-dollar companies like Coca-Cola, Pepsi Cola, Guinness—Diageo, Globacom, FirstBank, UBA, and Federal Inland Revenue Service.

He has proven turn-around successes in creating and directing high-profile marketing campaigns from inception to completion, conducting high-profile events and fostering professional relations (stakeholders, government, commercial) to meet organizational bottom-line objectives. He is adept and prominent in executing successful products/brands launches, instrumental in producing and distributing marketing materials, maintaining customer databases, and conducting market research to enhance overall business performance. He is an astute student of marketing, organizational development, and growth. He holds a BSc (Mass Communication), M.B.A, and MSc (Marketing) with several international and continental work experiences and exposures across Africa, Europe, Asia, the USA, and Canada. He retired as a Director of Corporate Communication with the Federal Inland Revenue Service and is currently the Managing Partner of DevaineBrands Consult Ltd.